# What I Wish I Had Heard
## Stories From Our Inner Child

Copyright © 2024 by Cassie Swift et al.

All rights reserved.

No portion of this book may be reproduced in any form without written permission from the publisher or author, except as permitted by UK copyright law.

This publication is designed to provide accurate and authoritative information in regard to the subject matter covered. It is sold with the understanding that neither the author nor the publisher is engaged in rendering legal, investment, accounting or other professional services. While the publisher and author have used their best efforts in preparing this book, they make no representations or warranties with respect to the accuracy or completeness of the contents of this book and specifically disclaim any implied warranties of merchantability or fitness for a particular purpose. No warranty may be created or extended by sales representatives or written sales materials. The advice and strategies contained herein may not be suitable for your situation. You should consult with a professional when appropriate. Neither the publisher nor the author shall be liable for any loss of profit or any other commercial damages, including but not limited to special, incidental, consequential, personal, or other damages.

**ISBN number for this book: 978-1-7396179-2-9**

Cover design by Heather Hulbert, www.heatherhulbert.co.uk

# Disclaimer

Please be aware that this book contains topics of a sensitive nature, some of which people may find upsetting or triggering. For permissions contact: cassie@trueyouchildrenslifecoaching.co.uk

This book is not intended to be a comprehensive medical guide. The opinions and information expressed in this publication are those of the authors only and they are sharing their expertise, but do not represent professional advice. This book is not intended as a substitute for seeking professional medical advice and the reader should regularly consult a medical expert in matters relating to their health, particularly with respect to any symptoms that might require a diagnosis or medical attention. The authors take no responsibility for any actions taken as a result of reading this book and do not assume and hereby disclaim any liability for any losses occurring as a result.

**Trigger warning:** please be advised that this book talks about issues that may be triggering, including CSA, eating disorders, self-harm, suicide attempts and abuse.

**I dedicate this book to all those little versions of us that have been made to feel inadequate and worthless. May these stories help you to look at, and maybe even begin healing, the innocent, amazing and precious little person inside of you still suffering!**

Listen along to each chapter as read by the author.
Just scan the QR code!

# Contents

1. Introduction — 1
   Cassie Swift

2. What We Do Not Repair, We Repeat — 9
   Jill Nicholson

3. Navigating The Depths Of Inner Healing: A Journey From Acrimonious Divorce To Rediscovering Trust And Self-Confidence — 23
   Kari Roberts

4. Resilience — 34
   Emma Starling

5. I'm not too much; I'm Neurodivergent — 42
   Nicola Reekie

6. Life Lessons for Young Adults — 51
   Clare Ford

7. From Darkness to Light: Overcoming Childhood Emotional Neglect — 59
   Kimberly Keane

| | | |
|---|---|---|
| 8. | The Day I Finally Chose To Evolve, Motivate, Inspire And Love You Emily<br>Emily Nuttall | 71 |
| 9. | Never Enough<br>Kertrina Gearing | 81 |
| 10. | I Wish I Had Known That I Was Not Alone<br>Annie Hunt | 88 |
| 11. | Author Bios: Cassie Swift | 99 |
| 12. | Jill Nicholson | 101 |
| 13. | Kari Roberts | 103 |
| 14. | Emma Starling | 105 |
| 15. | Nicola Reekie | 107 |
| 16. | Clare Ford | 109 |
| 17. | Kimberly Keane | 110 |
| 18. | Emily Nuttall | 111 |
| 19. | Kertrina Gearing | 112 |
| 20. | Annie Hunt | 114 |

# Introduction

# Cassie Swift

*'Only when we are brave enough to explore the darkness will we discover the infinite power of our light.'*
*– Brené Brown*

***Dedicated to Little Cassie; you will always be enough!***

Firstly thank you for picking up this book and opening the cover. Myself and the authors are all grateful and hope that this book will bring you comfort, and maybe even help you to begin your healing journey.

So what exactly is this book about and where did the idea come from?

This book contains the stories of ten incredible women who have been on a journey to connect with, and help, their 'inner child'.

Now I know there are many opinions with regards to work like this but not only have I experienced healing, I have witnessed many people make huge discoveries and transformations as a result of reconnecting and listening to the little version of them. In my opinion, it is some of the biggest and most fundamental work that you can do.

So what is the inner child?

The idea of the inner child is that it is your younger self within you, who still holds the beliefs from when you were a child growing up. The child you, the young person, the teen. When we are children, our brains aren't fully developed, and so the world can be interpreted in a very different way. This can result in beliefs being formed that aren't necessarily true, and it can play a part in the rest of our life.

Of course for some, there is childhood trauma, and that can further complicate what our view of the world is. In some circumstances severe trauma can actually impede emotional development and this is because it stops the ageing of our brains (to a certain extent) which means that a certain part of us will remain at a particular age that the traumatic event occurred, until it can be addressed and healed. This halt in brain development is not to say that the events themselves are not true, but more that the conclusions and decisions we make about ourselves, based on these events, are not.

So, the idea behind inner child work is that you are able to reconnect, re-engage, and gain the trust of your younger self. By doing that, you can start on the healing path. You can then act as an 'inner parent', if you will, and start re-parenting, helping and healing that part of you which has been hurt as a child. What you will find is that things like your self worth, your self esteem, your confidence, and your boundaries will in time become stronger. These are the thoughts and the beliefs that we adopt as children that affect how we grow up, our relationships with others, and our place within the world. So by healing this inner child part of us, we are able to heal and gain a different perspective on our experiences, instead of reverting back to the same narrative that we once did.

How did I work with the authors in this book?

Having been part of collaborative books and published my own in the past, I knew that this particular book concept was not just about the sharing of a story. That in itself is cathartic. By sharing your story, writing about it, and putting it out in the world it provides an element of healing yourself, as well as helping readers, by connecting and having empathy and understanding for one another. However, inner child work is very deep. So I knew that there had to be a further layer of support added. During this whole process, each of the authors have been offered Emotional Freedom Technique (EFT), along with other holistic therapies and energy work, which has helped to heal because it isn't just a one and done thing. It is very much a process.

Sometimes you can approach your inner child and they won't engage with you at all. This can be for various reasons. It could be because of severe trauma. It could be because that child was never listened to, so why should they engage now? There are often a variety of reasons, which is why this book was put together, specifically for the authors to heal. As a part of that they were then able to share their story so that you yourselves may realise how important this work is, and may even start your own healing journey with your inner child. Our hope is that you gain a lot out of this book and that the stories resonate with you.

As I began to think about this book and what to include I was trying to think of a specific event to write about, as I have done with other books. However, having done inner child work before, along with a lot of other healing I realised there was a pattern. I realised that all of the events that I'd shared with you in the past, and all the specific events that I was thinking about sharing here, have the same underlying theme.

To me, 'little me' regardless of what age I was when I was trying to connect to them, had the same recurring narrative:'I'm not good enough just being me'.

So not being enough as the real me, I was always having to be the good one, the quiet one, the perfect one. I was always being criticised for not doing something well enough, being told that I can and should do better, to not overreact, being ignored when I spoke, or not even being acknowledged at times. I was told I was weird, I was a nerd, a 'boff', a 'teacher's pet'. That was hard for me to actually accept, and I realised that all of this combined made 'little me' feel like there was something wrong with her! By being herself she wouldn't be enough, she wouldn't be liked, she wouldn't be accepted... she'd be rejected, she'd be abandoned and she'd be ignored!

As I write this, it is a harsh reality to face. It isn't a 'pity party', it is acknowledgement and realisation, and I feel so sorry for little Cassie.

Having these core beliefs that she was not enough is what did, and sometimes still does, shape my reality now. Experiencing love and meaningful relationships never happened because she felt she wasn't enough. She would mask and dissociate to make everything okay. She wouldn't have boundaries, because if you have boundaries it risks giving people an excuse to leave and an excuse to be unkind. She would continually strive for perfection, because anything less would result in more criticism. As I write my inner child is thinking about how I would get nine out of ten in a spelling test and there wouldn't be praise, instead: 'what happened to the other one?' I'd get a B in an exam and be asked why it's not an A. This went on and on. She would 'people please' all the time to keep the peace, to be liked, to be loved, and to avoid confrontation. This all started at a young age and continued right up into adulthood.

From a young age I knew I wasn't 'normal' in the sense of the word. I knew that I didn't fit in. The belief that I wasn't normal or enough ran through every scenario from family issues, to bullying and school issues. As did the belief that I had to change who I was, which drove me to academic perfection, masking on a daily basis just to be able to survive school, sixth form and uni, and ultimately drove me to burn out.

I did everything I could to 'fit in': being a good student, going to the toilets when everyone was smoking just because that was what the 'cool, popular' kids did. Being quiet at home to avoid arguments (and don't get me wrong this isn't in relation to my mum). My mum loved me so much. She wasn't perfect, but no mums are. I'm a mother and I'm far from perfect. She did her best.

Her overprotectiveness was a desire to stop me from getting hurt, and unfortunately not everyone in the house was like that. Everything I did and said would be wrong. Even when my parents split up there was still no interest, no acknowledgement. There were excuses not to see me and criticism of my schoolwork, no matter how hard I tried to be 'perfect'. All this did was reinforce the belief that I wasn't enough, that I wasn't important and wasn't wanted. All of this played a part in really low self esteem and continual perfectionism. It played a part in striving to be good enough. If I did well at school and got good reports, or I was recognised at awards evenings, then it was amazing. I'd get rewarded with 'things' not time (again not by my mum) but I wasn't happy. I went through most of my life with that underlying belief. The academic pressure all came to a head when I was nineteen and went to university.

So then my journey to recovery had to begin. At some point I addressed my inner child. At first I didn't want to, I didn't even know if it would work, and the idea that it would help at all seemed bizarre. It wasn't until I started doing this work and listening to 'little me', and I mean really, actively listening, building up the trust and reassurance that there would be no judgement or abandonment... just listening and accepting. I had to be really careful not to get caught up with regrets, and what I wish I'd done, or what could have happened differently, because I can't change the past and that would just be self torture. What was left for me to do was to decide how I could change the future.

It's still very much a work in progress, of building that bond, allowing myself the space and time, and I think this was the most difficult part—actually allowing myself to be a child. I grew up fast and I didn't have a lot of friends or playdates. So the concept of free childlike playing was quite bizarre. As I write this now I think about when I played with the My Little Ponies that I had. It's the only clear memory I have of free play. I didn't try to be 'perfect' at it, and I think even now, allowing myself to go back and be a child is something that I have to try and implement more. To jump in puddles, to have that carefree, judgement free, fun. Reminding myself that if you get muddy, it washes off. If the cookies get burnt, it doesn't matter. It doesn't mean that I'm wrong, or that there's something wrong with me. It means that I'm human and by letting my younger self know that, I can bring her comfort.

There are things that we're working on that I'm not going to share in detail at the moment. But by me being able to see things through a child's viewpoint and understanding this, I have been able to see that this was her perception of reality and was valid. In doing so it has allowed further healing to happen. I realise that when we talk about certain childhood events as adults they may seem totally stupid or irrational. However, as a child that's your reality. Your thoughts and beliefs are being formed in that time.

Again, we as young children don't grasp the concept that some situations aren't about us. In fact, as a child the world feels like it revolves around us. When things don't go right, we take it on board that it is our fault. That's how childhood and the child brain works. If that's not corrected at the time, these beliefs continue to develop and become ingrained. Again, that's not about bad parenting, ideas change over time which is then reflected in how different generations were raised. The thought pattern was that we were just children. We were told what to do and what not to do. We didn't really have many choices. It's not anything to do with people passing the blame, it's accepting that that is how it was, then empowering ourselves to learn ways to go back to start changing, acknowledging and moving on from these things.

Big changes can and will happen and I feel that the little me who was judged, abandoned, rejected—all she ever needed to hear was that she was loved for just being Cassie. She didn't have to be anybody else, didn't have to do anything else. Being her was perfect enough. So, to my younger self, what I wish I had heard is that no matter what happens, no matter who I am, I will always be unconditionally loved.

Which brings me to my wishes for you in reading this book. My hope is that by hearing about other people's inner child and the messages they have received from them, that you will want to embark on this special journey and get to hear a message of your very own!

But from me to you all, you are loved and you are enough, you always have been and always will be! XxX

# What We Do Not Repair, We Repeat

## Jill Nicholson

*'Trauma is the invisible force that shapes our lives. It shapes the way we live, the way we love and the way we make sense of the world. It is the root of our deepest wounds.'*
*- Dr Gabor Mate, The Wisdom of Trauma*

*I dedicate this chapter to the child parts within my siblings, of my clients past and present, in appreciation of the trust they have placed in me as their therapist. Finally, to my husband Paul, in whom I have the most loving*

***partner, friend and playmate, whose love continues to be such a healing force.***

The first time I heard of the concept of the 'inner child' I was twenty-two years old. It was in a book, which a friend had given me, about managing a physical condition I was living with. At the end of this helpful book was a short chapter on your inner child. I began to read it and I could feel the repulsion rise in me, so much so that, two pages into that chapter I tossed the book in the bin.

You would not be wrong in thinking this was an extreme and illogical reaction. I could not bear the concept that we had an inner child that was needy or sad. I refused to believe I had one inside myself! My numbness and stoicism left no room for any inner child shenanigans.

Remembering this now I am smiling at the extraordinary irony that can be woven into our paths. I am now fifty-six and I am very in touch with my inner child. I love her, play with her, and use her in my work. Even more ironic, if not hilarious, is the fact that I now work with the child part of others because I have been a counsellor and psychotherapist for the last twenty-four years (holy moly how did that happen?) The truth is my life's work has been all about empowering people to hear, witness and heal their inner child.

The kind of trauma I want to highlight in my chapter may be different from others. There was no abuse or a horrific event. The trauma I knew was the kind that was completely unintentional and probably unavoidable due to the situation. It was the 'drip..drip...drip' kind of chronic trauma throughout my childhood and teenage years until my early twenties, of living in the backdrop of my mum's mental health struggles and the impact of that.

I have been getting ahead of myself. Let's go back to the beginning.

I was born on the 9th of November 1967. The year the Beatles released 'Sgt. Pepper's Lonely Hearts Club Band', the Vietnam War was being fought, and Elvis Presley married Priscilla in Las Vegas.

I have three older siblings. We lived in a town half way between Edinburgh and Glasgow. My dad was fifty-two years old and my mum was forty. She believed she was menopausal but she was pregnant. Not just pregnant but pregnant with twins. My twin brother and I were born two months prematurely and we both weighed under three pounds. We were in incubators and it was touch and go over the first few days. My eldest brother described us as 'looking like skinned rabbits'. We were scrawny and skinny. My mum wanted to call us Jack and Jill, fortunately, my dad suggested we would not get through school alive. Jack became Andrew but Jill stuck. I am a Jill not a Jillian. Being a twin has been one of the biggest blessings throughout my life. We were premature babies. We had to be fed every two hours and my mum's mum, Grandma B, moved in to help. It must have been so hard and exhausting.

There was a story in my family that I was a 'dour' baby. Dour is a Scottish word which means sullen or moody. I did not crack a smile until I was six months old, until my great Uncle Bill leaned over our pram, talking to us and making faces, and I smiled and laughed for the first time. When my mum recounted this story to me as a child she told me that she was afraid that her depression while she was pregnant with us had affected me. Early on as a sensitive child I wondered if I was a bit faulty in some way. I made sure to smile a lot but often it was a smile that didn't come from inside.

I loved the security and the 'belonging' of being in a big family. It was a very traditional family. My dad had a business as a gentlemen's outfitter and my mum, who had been a physiotherapist, stopped work when she married. Looking back we often wondered if this choice (that was the norm in 1961) had been the wrong one for her. Perhaps like many professional women of her time, she experienced the joy of marriage and motherhood, but equally lost herself in a way that created vulnerability. My dad had been born in 1915 to a family that did not express emotions or show affection. A common emotional climate at that time. He was the youngest of five and was used to the 'rough and tumble' of family life and sibling relationships in a way that my mum was not. My mum, who was twelve years younger than my dad, was an only child born into a very loving family who easily showed emotion.

It is not hard to see how there might have been challenges in being with each other. Ultimately, how we attach to others is dictated by the 'blueprint' we learn from our caregivers. I have never met a human being for whom this is not true. Fortunately, we can change that 'blueprint' sometimes through life or parenthood, sometimes through getting help to reshape it.

One of my earliest and 'sorest' memories I have of my mum occurred not long after my twin and I started school. We were dressing for school and our mum was slumped on the floor in her dressing gown crying, saying: "I can't do this anymore. I want to die."

As an empathic child I didn't just see her pain, I could feel it. I tried to comfort her but she was beyond that in a bubble of depression and despair. We all make conclusions from our experiences as a child. They are usually unconscious. Looking back as an adult, I could see the jigsaw of experiences that formed my attachment style, vulnerabilities, strengths, and my view of myself, others, and the world.

Four-and-a-half year old me took in what was happening and made decisions and conclusions, such as: I was not good enough because I could not help her, and that in some way I was responsible for how she felt. Here's the important part to understand… these decisions and conclusions were made with a child's lack of cognition, lack of reasoning and lack of power. There were hundreds of 'sore' situations like that one with Mum in our childhood.

This is not a judgement on anyone, it is just a fact. It was also a fact for my parents. They each formed their attachment styles, vulnerabilities, strengths and views of themselves, others and the world in their earliest years with a child's cognitive and emotional capacity. This was also a fact for all generations that came before them.

What we do not repair, we repeat.

They did and I did.

Perhaps you are repeating yours too.

# 'Life can only be understood backwards, but it must be lived forwards'
# - Søren Kierkegaard

Now, before I continue, I want to state something with utter clarity and conviction. This understanding of how our parents or caregivers personalities were carved out can be really helpful.

However, there is an exception.

If you have experienced abuse of any form, understanding the perpetrator is NOT your job. You have been injured and that is not okay, end of story. For some clients I've worked with, understanding the context of abuse can be helpful, but this is not the case for everyone. You are the only person that you can heal. Healing you is a matter of the greatest importance. The quality of your future depends on it.

A crucial factor in healing our inner child is to understand that it operates with the cognitive and emotional capacity of a young child. So many of the unconscious beliefs we hold and the conclusions we make are distorted and quite frankly 'wonky' (not a clinical term). Furthermore, it is from these unconscious beliefs, that we live our lives. Simply put, for many of us, that young, wounded child is in the driving seat of our lives. Yikes!

So what hidden and deeply 'filed away' conclusions did I come to in my young mind? That:

- I was bad in some way to have caused my mum such distress.

- I was not 'good enough' because I could not make it better.

- Life was not safe and it was scary. I was not sure what 'to die' meant at that age but I knew it was bad and that mum might not be there when I got home from school.

- I was responsible for her distress and therefore had to help her.

The self-betrayal happened early. My mum had lost herself, and I was about to lose myself before I had really found out who I was. I became a people pleaser, a perfectionist, a person without emotional needs. My fear was swallowed down. I learned to be numb.

You know the story of Pinocchio, the wooden boy who wanted to be real. In many ways I became a wooden girl: numb and pleasing, but not quite real.

I was a child who hid any 'negative' feelings like sadness and fear. I was a child who thought about the consequences of actions too early. I was a child who put others first, before I had learned about my own needs. I was a child who did not express anger but turned it inwards, flipping it round to believe it must be me who was at fault (a very common one for kids to do if they do not feel safe enough to be angry at parents). I was a child who felt responsible for keeping people safe without actually knowing how to do it for myself. I was a teenager who did not rebel, by this I mean I did not kick against boundaries. However, that teenage rebellion has an important development function and is crucial for the process Carl Jung called 'individuation'. In this process we separate from our caregivers' ideologies and expectations and find our own uniqueness. In doing so, we hopefully learn that we are acceptable, loved and safe as our true, authentic self.

But perhaps the biggest impact was that I did not have a sense of emotional safety. I became an anxious child without ever showing it. I found a way to comfort that anxiety by emotional eating. At the age of twenty I weighed twenty stone. My persona was that of 'Jolly Jilly' who inside was not really jolly at all. I was numb.

Another way to describe numbness is to freeze and I would often feel shutdown. My nervous system was used to being in 'fight or flight' but we can only stay there for so long before a switch is tripped and we are dropped down into a freeze response. Being emotionally dysregulated became familiar. I have spent so much of my adult life finding ways to regulate my nervous system and find a sense of feeling 'inner safety'; a state where one is neither in 'fight or flight' or in 'freeze' on a continual loop.

I was really blessed with elder siblings who did so much with us, particularly our eldest sister who took us on so many days out and holidays and mothered us. At the age of four I was allowed into her bedroom. It contained so many treasures! Treasures like false eyelashes, high heels, lipstick, and nail varnish. I would watch her transfixed as she got ready for a night out, putting on her make-up, with 'Bye Bye Miss American Pie' by Don McLean playing in the background.

My eldest brother took me to a library when I was little and started my love of reading. Then as I got older, it was just my middle sister, twin brother and I at home with mum and dad. When mum was hospitalised due to her declining mental health, we formed a trio, coping with what the day brought as we waited for her to be well enough to come home. We wondered which version of Mum would return to us. My middle sister's laughter and levity brightened many of those dark days.

My beloved dad's emotional capacity was not well suited to the situation we all found ourselves in. He did his best. We all did. He taught us about tenacity and instilled in us a 'joie de vivre' and an appreciation of life's simple pleasures, like playing a card game together.

My twin and I had the most powerful and beautiful experience of my mum when we were in our early twenties. For the first time, this woman that Dad and her friends had spoken about appeared. She became well. She and my dad fit together in a way I had not seen before. This funny, erudite woman, who had a line of poetry for every situation, who played the piano and sang, who had a naughty sense of humour and was loving, arrived. She noticed our feelings.

One cherished memory is my twin and I at our mum and dad's house one evening. We had given her a white, fluffy bunny toy at Easter. She was playing with it, making it talk, sing and dance as we sat cross-legged at her feet engrossed in the show our mummy was performing for us. At the age of twenty-three in our young adulthood, we had the most healing childhood experience with our mum. It was glorious beyond words.

Our time with this amazing woman who had arrived so late was too short. Two years later she died. I left the hospice where she died and walked to my car and I remember experiencing a feeling like all the colour in the world had gone. Everything seemed dull. She had brought such colour to our lives in these last two years. Thank God, we had these years. They were such a gift. She remains to this day one of my most favourite human beings I have ever encountered.

In my own therapy I began my healing journey. I experienced liberation and deep, deep sadness. Then came the excruciating fear that had always been in there. I remember saying to my therapist that I felt as if the 'Jaws music' was always playing in my head. It was hell. It was necessary. I was at last taking off that 'anaesthetic coating' which created the numbness. I began to feel. At the age of thirty, the wooden girl was becoming real.

I guess I started rebuilding the woman I wanted to be. The woman I could be when the 'blueprints' were challenged and updated. I did this with a remarkable and wise therapist. With her I 're-grew up'. You might have gathered from my story that I wasn't a child for long enough. The child part of me had been dormant as I tried to control my world.

I remember drawing in one session. I think it was about awakening the child part of me. She said it was time to round up the session and stop drawing. Without looking up I said, "NO THANK YOU... I don't want to stop". She clapped her hands and laughed shouting, "here's your free child... hooray!" I did not consider it might be rude of me to say that. I did not think it might inconvenience her, or make her late for her next client. All I felt was the fun of the drawing and that I WAS NOT READY TO STOP. It was a milestone.

Some of the emotional development stages that I had missed as a child, I redid with her. For example, reworking the people pleasing, the perfectionism and comfort eating. I no longer carried the unspoken trauma and sadness on my body in the form of pounds.

She really was the re-making of me. Or maybe it was the return to myself. Maybe both. She was a light for me and it is with her I started to find a sense of inner safety. I truly understood the concept of the inner child. She used a set of Russian nesting dolls in our work together, to illustrate a complex psychological principle so simply. Inside the big one is a smaller one, and then another and another. With her I learned how to dialogue with my inner child and I at last heard the younger parts of myself.

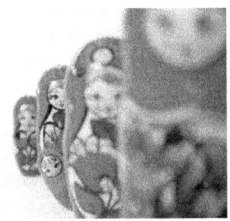

I use Russian nesting dolls in my work with clients when appropriate, and I always tell them who I learned this technique from. What a therapeutic gift she gave me.

Feeling safe 'inside' has been a big one for me. I would achieve that safety and then life events like a divorce would trigger me back to standing in the shoes of that frightened child, who believed she was inadequate or faulty in some way.

Here's an interesting side point - for me the changes in hormones in menopause, at times, brought the return of that feeling and I needed to look after that child part of me even more and attend to her with greater gusto.

My therapist showed me the kind of therapist I wanted to be. I specifically trained in Transactional Analysis which has simple frameworks which rebalance the parts of us which are over or underactive such as the self critical part or the free child part.

Trauma is not what happens to us but what happens inside us due to our experiences.

We cannot change what happened to us. It is part of our history. We cannot make trauma 'unhappen'.

My deepest hope is that you take away from this chapter the fact that: we can change what happens inside us now, that is the sweet spot where healing can take place.

Working with clients is and remains one of the greatest joys in my life. I have developed a way of working that is laser focused in getting to the root of the difficulties, to start that much needed healing. I know that journey personally and professionally. I know how powerfully it can transform people and change the futures they create. It changed mine beyond measure.

If you or someone you know is frightened that you need to talk about all your trauma, please find a therapist who can start by pinpointing your trauma in a way that does not always require you to retell it. Not re-traumatising clients is so important. Our 'stuff' is evident in our everyday life. In my past, the people pleasing part of me could be seen in my actions and choices. In the same way that our DNA is present in every cell, the impact of our trauma can show up in our present.

Escaping the shadow of our pasts is complex and tiring work. It walks the duality of being heartbreaking and heart-mending... but it is possible.

As I bid you goodbye, I bring back to me all the younger parts of myself that I have introduced you to. I gather them up lovingly. They did their very best, they found a way to survive and I thank them for it. I look on them with kindness.

They are safe with me now.

Wonderfully, I am married to a man, Paul, who is open to my strengths and vulnerabilities, to my sorted-ness and my wobbliness. I am deeply seen and heard. I am utterly grateful for such a partner and playmate. He has been another unexpected layer of my healing.

I want to share a little secret with you. As a client's inner child finds healing, my inner child is jumping with joy and cheering them on from the side lines. She knows what it means to find freedom and she feels their happiness.

Isn't life strange? The sensitive, fearful, empathic, little girl became a wooden girl. The wooden girl eventually became a real girl who became a real woman. Then the real woman healed her inner child more and became a therapist. This therapist now has the honour of empowering and accompanying other people's injured child parts to healing and freedom.

I read this back and think 'what a deliciously ironic story'. I have found peace.

Life so far has taught me that there is always a way through, we just need to find it.

May the child parts within you be seen, heard, healed and loved.

Xx

***'You are braver than you believe, stronger than you seem, and smarter than you think but the most important thing is, even if we're apart...***

*I'll always be with you.'*
*- Winnie the Pooh*

# Navigating The Depths Of Inner Healing: A Journey From Acrimonious Divorce To Rediscovering Trust And Self-Confidence

## Kari Roberts

*'Within every adult, there resides the heart of a child. Healing the inner child is the key to unlocking the potential for joy, creativity, and resilience in our lives.'*
— *Wayne W. Dyer*

*This chapter is dedicated to my six year old self. To the boundless imagination and endless curiosity that filled your heart. Remember the world is filled with endless possibilities waiting to be discovered. May this chapter inspire you to ask questions, dream big, and embrace the beauty of curiosity.*

## Acrimonious Divorce

As the sun dipped below the horizon, casting long shadows across the sky, my father took me back to my mother's holding onto my hand tightly. I can still feel the anxiety fill every part of my body when I recall this. My mother grabbed me and threw me through the door. My eyes, wide with fear, darted between my bickering parents. Their words and the shouting echoed in my six year old heart, unconsciously leaving an indelible mark on me. I can still hear the front door slam and the sense of despair as I sat in the hallway for hours until being dragged to bed, even fifty-four years later. That is the power of trauma and the impact on the inner child.

Divorce is never easy, and when it descends into acrimony, the scars run deep, especially for the children caught in the crossfire. My journey toward healing is paved with understanding, compassion, and actionable steps to reclaim my lost sense of self.

## The Shattered Innocence

My story is not unique. Acrimonious divorce, marked by bitterness, shatters the innocence of countless children. The emotional turmoil, witnessing parental disputes left an indelible mark on my psyche and on many others. The inner child—that pure and unblemished essence within—becomes wounded, casting a long shadow into adulthood, having an impact on every relationship I have had, especially my relationship with myself.

## Trust Issues: The Lingering Echo

Trust is the cornerstone of healthy relationships, but for children scarred by acrimonious divorces, it becomes a fragile commodity. The betrayal of trust creates a blueprint for the child's understanding of relationships. I now know that as I grew, I found myself questioning the intentions of those around me, always anticipating the next betrayal. In many cases I sabotaged them before the betrayal.

The echoes of my parents' divorce reverberate in my mind, causing me to view the world through a lens of suspicion. Trust became a delicate dance, a step forward inevitably followed by a hesitant retreat. Rebuilding this shattered trust has been a delicate process, one that required so much introspection and conscious effort.

## Low Self-Confidence: A Silent Erosion

The battleground of divorce is no place for a child, yet they often find themselves in the crossfire. I observed my parents tearing each other apart (mainly fuelled by my mother's needs and my father's fear of losing contact with me) while internalising their discord. The toxic environment eroded my self-esteem, leaving me with lingering doubts about my worth.

Low self-confidence becomes the silent companion of children from tumultuous divorces. As an adult I was second-guessing my abilities, downplaying every achievement, and self sabotaging relationships. The scars of my childhood linger in the way that, even now, I hesitate to speak up, fearing rejection, shame and judgement.

## Nurturing My Inner Child: A Path to Healing

Reclaiming the inner child was a pivotal step towards healing from the wounds of my childhood. Understanding the impact of the past was the first stride towards a brighter future. As you continue to read this, stay with me while I attempt to explore my transformative journey learning to mend the broken pieces and rediscover the things I lost from my childhood. A caveat here: this is an ongoing journey, even at sixty years old I still catch myself. One question I always ask myself when I wobble is 'how am I self sabotaging?'

As I continue I share some of the steps I employed in my healing. Some I acquired through counselling, others through personal experience. While I've arranged them in a particular order, it's important to note that they do not need to be experienced in this specific chronology.

## Acknowledging the Pain

My journey began with recognising and acknowledging the pain. I first confronted the deep-seated wounds from my childhood in my early thirties when my role as a parenting expert provided personal centred counselling. The counsellor became a guide, helping me navigate the tumultuous landscape of emotions. Through tears and revelations, I began to unravel the knots of my past, allowing the healing process to commence. Every session resulted in me sobbing loudly but feeling weightless by the end. It took me a while to lower my armour to see that acknowledging the pain was not a sign of weakness, rather, a testament of strength. It requires courage to confront the ghosts of the past, to peel back the layers of hurt and confront the scars head-on. This acknowledgement laid the foundation for rebuilding a shattered sense of self. It was the beginning of the next steps.

1. Cultivating Self-Compassion

    As I delved deeper into therapy, I learnt the art of self-compassion. What really helped was not continually looking back, but looking forward to how I wanted to feel and for life to look. The inner child, wounded and fragile, yearns for gentleness and understanding. I was able to nurture my inner child, offering the love and care that was lacking in my formative years.

    Cultivating self-compassion is a balm for the wounded soul. It involves embracing one's vulnerabilities with kindness, recognising that the scars do not define the person. I learnt to speak to myself with the same compassion I offered others, breaking the cycle of self-criticism that has plagued me for years. In doing this I was able to cultivate understanding and compassion for my parents and find a sense of forgiveness which brought peace.

2. Rebuilding Trust: A Gradual Unfolding

Trust, once shattered, cannot be rebuilt overnight. For me, the journey towards trusting others began with trusting myself. Through small, consistent steps, I learnt to rely on my instincts and judgement. Ongoing counselling provided a safe space for me to explore these new facets of trust, slowly expanding my comfort zone.

Rebuilding trust involves setting boundaries and learning to communicate assertively. I discovered that trust is not an all-or-nothing concept. It is a gradual unfolding, a nuanced dance between vulnerability and resilience. As I learnt to trust myself, the walls around my heart began to crumble, allowing genuine connections to take root.

3. Fostering Positive Relationships

The impact of acrimonious divorce on a child's understanding of relationships is profound. Armed with newfound self-awareness, I ventured into the realm of building positive connections. By surrounding myself with individuals who uplift and support me it allowed me to see that I wanted to have a family that counterbalances the tumult of my past.

Fostering positive relationships involves discernment and a willingness to let go of toxic connections. I am now able to identify red flags and set healthy boundaries, creating a protective circle that nurtures my growth. As I forge bonds built on trust and respect, the scars of my past slowly fade, replaced by the warmth of genuine connection.

## Tools for Healing: Practical Steps Towards Wholeness

The one thing I am sure of is that a journey of healing is not a solitary one. It's a collaborative effort, requiring practical tools and steps that can guide towards reclaiming your inner child and fostering a robust sense of trust and self-confidence. Some of these are:

## Therapeutic Interventions

Therapy has emerged as a cornerstone in the healing process. Professional therapists provide a safe and non-judgmental space for individuals to explore their emotions, unravel the complexities of their past, and develop coping mechanisms for the present. There are various therapeutic modalities, such as cognitive-behavioural therapy (CBT), dialectical behaviour therapy (DBT), eye movement desensitisation and reprocessing (EMDR), which offer tailored approaches to healing.

Group therapy becomes a powerful avenue for shared experiences and collective healing. This can be scary and I know I would have run away from this in the beginning. However, in a group setting I have experienced solace in realising I was not alone. It wasn't just me, and if it wasn't just me, then this wasn't personal. The shared narratives of triumph and resilience create a supportive tapestry that aids in breaking the prison of feeling isolated by shame.

## Mindfulness Practices

Mindfulness, rooted in ancient practices like meditation and deep breathing, can offer a transformative path towards healing for some. I initially struggled with this, but after realising it was just about taking notice and being present, I discovered the profound impact of mindfulness on my emotional well-being. Mindful breathing becomes an anchor, grounding you in moments of anxiety. Through regular practice, you can learn to observe thoughts without judgement, cultivating a sense of inner calm.

Mindfulness practices extend beyond meditation. They encompass activities that bring joy and presence. Engaging in hobbies, dancing, savouring a delicious meal, or walking my dog in nature has become a form of mindfulness for me. These practices, woven into the fabric of daily life, contributed to the gradual restoration of my inner child.

## Journaling

The act of journaling is such a powerful therapeutic tool for self-reflection. I began to journal my thoughts and emotions, tracing the patterns of my inner narrative. Journaling provided me with a tangible record of my growth, serving as a compass in moments of self-doubt.

Through reflective writing, you can explore the roots of trust issues and low self-confidence. It becomes a dialogue with the inner child, unravelling the layers of pain and fostering a compassionate understanding of yourself. The process of putting pen to paper becomes a cathartic release, allowing emotions to flow freely and paving the way for healing.

In his book 'Think Again', Adam Grant talks about the importance of challenging what we think. In my journaling I would ask myself questions specifically about thinking and cognitive processes. It allowed me to connect with my thought processes, for example questions like:

- What do I notice about my thinking?
- How often have I thought that thought?
- How can I think differently?

I find these questions really helpful when I feel really stuck or didn't know when I feel emotionally charged.

## Empowerment through Education

Knowledge is power, and in the journey towards healing education becomes a potent tool. I opened myself to reading and resources that explored the psychological impacts of acrimonious divorces on children. Understanding the dynamics of trauma and its ripple effects empowered me to break free from the chains of generational patterns.

These resources extended to workshops, seminars, and support groups. I discovered the value of learning from experts in the field and connecting with others who share similar experiences. Empowerment through education becomes a beacon of hope, which guides you towards informed choices and a deeper understanding of your own narratives.

## Building a Supportive Network

It is really hard to travel the path of healing in isolation. Building a supportive network becomes a crucial aspect of the journey. Once hesitant, if not adamant not to share my struggles, I soon learnt the power of reaching out. The strength of communal support lies in its ability to validate experiences and provide a safety net during moments of vulnerability.

Support networks may extend to online communities, where people from diverse backgrounds share their stories and offer words of encouragement. Virtual spaces become platforms for connection, breaking down geographical barriers and fostering a global community of healing. Through these networks, you may discover that the reclamation of the inner child is a collective endeavour, woven into the tapestry of shared resilience.

## Conclusion: A Journey of Rediscovery

As I continue my journey of healing by writing this I reflect on the distance I have travelled. The scars of acrimonious divorce no longer define me, they are but a testament to my strength and resilience. The inner child, once wounded and cowering, now stands tall, bathed in the light of self-love and acceptance and forgiveness.

The impact of acrimonious divorce on trust issues and low self-confidence is profound, but it is not insurmountable. Through acknowledging the pain, cultivating self-compassion, and rebuilding trust, I have reclaimed my inner child and set forth on a path towards wholeness.

The tools for healing, from therapeutic interventions to mindfulness practices and education, provide a roadmap for navigating the intricate terrain of emotional recovery. Building a supportive network becomes the scaffolding that holds individuals upright during moments of vulnerability.

The journey towards healing is not linear; it is a dynamic process marked by setbacks and triumphs. Each step, no matter how small, contributes to the transformation of the inner child. As the shadows of the past recede, you emerge into the light of self-discovery, embracing the fullness of its potential.

I am reminded of a tapestry while drawing this chapter to an end, a tapestry of healing, the reclamation of the inner child is a masterpiece—a testament to the indomitable spirit within each individual. Everyday I take steps towards my newfound self, the self that I have always been from the moment I was born, knowing that I am enough. I know that my story is not just mine alone; it is a beacon of hope for others navigating the tumultuous waters of acrimonious divorce—both adults and children. The journey is ongoing, but the destination is one of rediscovery, empowerment, and the triumphant emergence of a healed soul.

# Resilience

# Emma Starling

*'Until you make the unconscious conscious, it will direct your life and you will call it fate'*
*- Carl Jung*

**To all those who have struggled to love themselves, this is for you.**

I could see them all skipping and I really wanted to join in. They motioned me over and jumped into the ropes, immediately getting it wrong. The instant embarrassment rose inside me like a nauseating tidal wave and I walked away. I was new here, and didn't have any friends. They had all been left behind at my previous school. I don't know what else it could have been but all of a sudden things just felt... different. I felt lost much of the time, my gaze mostly downwards and a feeling of deep abandonment swallowed whole days.

I can't describe it any way other than I just knew that they all disliked me and it pricked my skin. Standing in the playground I could see the two popular sisters. They had lived in America, had long blonde hair and looked like Barbie dolls. Their dresses were so pretty, and their shoes made me jealous—especially on school photograph day. I don't remember ever looking like that and it didn't feel fair. I can remember the school dinners being really nice and we were able to serve ourselves on each table. The yummy puddings made me feel better about all the times I didn't compare to the other girls, but soon that made things even worse.

I pulled on a pair of size twelve, hand-me-down jeans and was bursting out of them, aged eight or nine. I couldn't do sports and was not particularly good at maths. I just didn't get it. Art and more creative things were my better subjects and I did have a friend in one particular teacher. She was firm but kind and she always encouraged me, no matter what.

Coming up to the school sports day, the child who was due to run the two-hundred metre race became poorly and they wanted someone to fill in. I offered, along with some others. Miss Smith, my favourite teacher, trialled us that afternoon and whoever won would run in the race. The starter gun went off and we all started running. I got going well but after about five seconds I ran out of steam, and as all the other girls overtook me, that familiar shame welled up and I pretended to fall over for an excuse, aside from just being rubbish. Everyone was laughing. How did I ever think I could do that? How could I measure up to everyone else?

When I was nine my grandma died suddenly while I was away on a school trip. I came home and she was gone. My best friend and safe place. It tore me up inside. I stood in assembly while the others sang the day's hymn, and I couldn't even get my breath. I felt so very lost and alone and sank deeper into the solace that food gave me.

One day, I was lined up in the library waiting to play a netball match with my old school when I heard sniggering. I turned around to see a group of my old friends standing not too far away, and just loud enough for me to hear, they giggled and said: "that's Emma, hasn't she got fat!"

I'm sure my face went crimson and I started to cry. They used to be my friends, why were they being so mean? I don't remember anything about the game after that, I was consumed with horrible, sharp feelings of shame and humiliation that wouldn't go away.

That, and many other experiences like it, planted the seed that I wasn't good enough. From being verbally bullied to humiliated on a daily basis, to being publicly broken up with by my first boyfriend in the playground—everything just kept ticking that box.

Not good enough. Not pretty enough. Not clever enough. Not thin enough.

One Saturday morning when I was about thirteen, I came downstairs in my nightdress, sat on the couch and cried. There was nothing particular that had happened that morning but those tears had been welling up inside me ever since we moved schools when I was seven. I couldn't stop.

There was no explanation I could give for my tears and therefore no comfort could be given. The tears stopped and went back down inside.

At this point, I decided to take control of my eating so I could lose weight. I would typically have one small bread roll at lunchtime and then some noodles for tea. One day at my sister's flat, we had just finished Sunday dinner and I went to the loo. I returned to questions about what I had been doing and whether I had been purging. I didn't realise how thin I had become and when I sat and thought about it, I realised I had not had a period for a couple of months. That jolt of fear coupled with the worry I was causing my family ended my starvation style diet then and there.

In the years that followed, I would lose some weight, gain some weight and repeat the cycle. In hindsight, I think I was punishing myself for not being good enough, then proving to myself that I was right. I think I was thirty-six by the time I realised why this had all started happening.

Moving away from all my friends, and losing my grandma not long after that, were the two catalyst points that drove much of my life, until I realised what was happening.

When I was seventeen, I tried reflexology and found it incredibly soothing. I had never been one to find comfort in Western medicine or the traditional way of taking a pill to feel better. Something about the effect this had on me rippled out through my whole body. I was hooked.

It was a long journey between this moment and my discovery of the thing that would change my life trajectory forever. Aged thirty-six I discovered I was an empath. I learned all about my sensitivity and the reason I just knew stuff I couldn't explain. A sigh of relief spread through my body, mind and energy field as I realised—I wasn't neurotic, or paranoid. I was claircognizant and had a very strong sense of inner knowing, without knowing how I knew.

Suddenly, all the friendships I had lost over the years made sense. I knew they were lying. They didn't know how I could possibly know, so branded me paranoid and the friendship drifted. All the times people's words felt like knives flying at me had been softened by the weight I had amassed to protect myself. I felt seen and validated for probably the first time in my life. Again, I dove deeper.

Studying with Wendy Da Rosa, an expert guide for empaths, helped me understand what had happened, and the impact everything had had on my nervous system and chakras. I felt so fundamentally unable to be myself that I had contracted at root and sacral level. That impact had rippled its way up through the rest of my energy centres, sapping me of my power to speak up, or take action on anything.

As a child I never knew about anything like that, but as an adult, with my knowledge of traditional Chinese medicine and reflexology behind me, it made total sense.

The next epiphany was when I discovered the Emotional Freedom Technique. This became the thing that completely turned my life around, and freed me from the shackles I'd been living under. If that sounds overly dramatic I assure you it isn't. I can clearly remember the first time I came across it. It looked and sounded way too simple to be effective, and even I wondered if it was just smoke and mirrors. Then I tapped.

In that moment when I first learned to use EFT, it was like everything that had ever trapped me, began to melt away. Not all in one go, of course, but I could feel that this was the beginning of something that would set me free. I felt lighter, the burdens of my childhood gently dissolving away like butterflies.

As my journey with EFT went deeper, I also discovered Inner Child Work. This was the way I discovered that I could actually go back and soothe the little me, the way she needed to be soothed. All mammals need co-regulation with other mammals and when that isn't present at the time it's needed, it creates trauma, and can shut you down at root chakra level and beyond. In order to re-parent and nurture that inner child, we need to acknowledge, without judgement, that there would have been tons of those occasions in our childhood (unless our parents were experts in holistic psychology).

A few years ago, I studied to be an oracle using Soul Plan techniques by Blue Marsden, to figure out my soul's destiny. It further opened my eyes to why I was on this journey to become a 'master builder' of communities. You see, we all carry energy within the frequency of the letters in our names that contribute to this journey, and mine are showstoppers.

I have codes about abundance and flow, healing the heart, being a mirror for others, and emotional resilience. As I stared at the report, everything once again clicked into place. I was exactly where I was meant to be to get where I'm going, and I have all of the gifts and talents needed to transmute any challenges into gold on the way there.

I had to learn about the depths of emotions to be able to hold the level of joy that I do today. I had to learn about how awful it was to be frozen in inertia before I could help people to heal, and move into flow and abundance. I had to be subjected to the emotions of others so that I could learn how to be a mirror for them to heal. I had to go through so much pain and rejection so that I could learn resilience. I had to feel so alone in order to build communities that are my hallmark today. I had to experience so much rejection so that I could learn to accept myself completely. I had to experience debt and lack to fully appreciate abundance and flow.

I learnt about the beauty and power of frequency and vibration, and the universal laws that govern us all, so that I could bring that knowledge to others in a grounded and relatable way, pulling on my own experiences. I came here to be a bringer of higher truths that can set people free from their own shackles, just as they released me from mine.

To my inner child, I say this: you were always perfect in your perceived imperfections. They were exactly what you needed to bring you to this point. You are stronger because of them and you are a leader because you healed from them. You give me inspiration when I look back and think about the road you have travelled, how you dealt with the pain that came your way. I am so very proud of you for how you handled yourself and how you had the courage to walk your own path. You and I didn't come here to conform. We came here to shed light on things that others can't. We came here to share our wisdom and resilience with others, and everything you experienced led you to the tools I use now. You're with me every step of the way because I hold you inside my heart. I love you so very much and you have never not deserved to receive your heart's desire. I'm so sorry you went through the pain, and I'm so glad you stayed the course to get us here. I'm so sorry you lost so much, and I'm so proud of the person you have become. Your heart was always as pure as your intention. You can truly be grateful for all that's happening, because you have so much personal power later in your life, and you lead with compassion and empathy for those going through the same.

You could never have known this at the time, but you came here to start a movement. To spread the ripple of energy work through the planet, and to train others in the same skills you developed. You could never have anticipated the impact those skills would have on the lives of others. Your healing ripple is only just beginning. I am still healing even now, aged forty-eight, but this time there is no confusion about why things are happening, and no shame about my feelings. You were loved then, you are loved now. I see you, I love you, I AM you, and you are such a beautiful soul. Never doubt how precious you are, little one. Your presence here is so very needed.

I hope this chapter has been useful for anyone who reads it, and if you would make peace with your past as you forge an exciting new future, I would love to chat with you. In the meantime, I will leave you with the two quotes that sum up my journey thus far, in the hope that they spark something in you as they did in me.

> ***'Without the heart, there can be no understanding between the hand and the mind.'***
> ***- Anon.***

I am here for you. We are one. I love you.

# I'm not too much; I'm Neurodivergent

## Nicola Reekie

*'I'm not too much, I'm neurodivergent'*
*- Nicola Reekie*

*To all of those who self-identify as autistic or neurodivergent having grown up in a world that made no sense. To Karen who turned my voice notes into the written word. For all of those who are self diagnosed or on this journey. To all of the speakers who have spoken within the PDA space who have contributed to my work and my own personal development.*

# WHAT I WISH I HAD HEARD

This is the story of my journey from being the child that was 'too much', through teenage years of risk-taking, to an acceptance in adulthood of my own neurodivergence.

I will use the term neurodivergent to cover my experiences related to the following different needs: dyslexia, dyspraxia, autism and ADHD. It has taken perhaps forty years for my distressed inner child to understand that none of this was ever my fault.

My brain is wired differently than the norm. I am unique. My brain responds to stimuli in ways that affect my perception and my communication, overloading my senses, causing anxiety and difficulty with 'doing' life. My perception and communication difficulties were very evident in my family life, education and socialising.

There are many things I wish that I had understood as a child growing up but, more importantly, I wish that my family, my caregivers and educators had understood them. I dearly wish that they had had the skills and expertise to respond to my challenges by teaching me coping strategies, and treating me with love and compassion.

Instead, I was blamed for everything, gaslighted by everyone, and told everything was my fault. I was told I was too loud, too demanding, too whiny, and too much this and that. Consequently, my mental health and wellbeing suffered. I constantly felt weird, that I was wrong, that somehow everyone else had the rulebook of life apart from me. I just didn't get it.

As a child, I was frequently sick but there was never an obvious reason why. I really struggled with noise, and still do. I find it nearly impossible to filter out other noises. For example, if I am in a busy cafe, concentrating on the conversation with the person I'm sitting with is impossible. The majority of people can block out other noise; I can't. A school environment is also very noisy, so when there were numerous conversations going on, I could never discern which one to listen to, and which to filter out.

I was never quite sure what I should be listening to, or who I should pay attention to when in a small group at playtime or during social activities. This meant that I never quite knew how to interpret any form of communication, and thus a whole swathe of social niceties and nuances passed me by. It has taken a lot of work to really understand them, if I even really do now.

I could not process things as quickly as others and would often misunderstand what was going on. I felt constantly overwhelmed. One coping strategy I adopted was to mimic others around me, but my peers at school would tease or bully me, accusing me of copying them.

By the time I had formulated what I wanted to say to share my own ideas, I was unable to communicate clearly as the appropriate moment had passed and I would slip into a trauma response. I will expand on trauma responses later in my chapter.

Another thing I was aware of, but again didn't understand, was clothing. Why did certain clothing feel wrong, itchy and so uncomfortable? I stopped doing many activities because I didn't like the clothing. I still, to this day, remember being four years old and hating the leotard I had to wear for ballet because it felt tight on my arms. I grew up in an era where Aran jumpers were a big thing and jeans were very heavy and thick. I found these to be most uncomfortable. At the same time, I kept many of my favourite items of clothing for years and years, simply because I liked how they felt. At the time I didn't understand why. When I was old enough, at the age of thirteen, I started a newspaper round to earn money so that I could choose my own clothes that felt comfortable to wear. That made a big difference to my sensory experience.

I found food and eating difficult as a child. I have strong memories of head teachers' wagging fingers at me, telling me to "just eat it, why can't you eat it?" At the time, I was overwhelmed by being in a noisy lunch hall. I also struggled with the physical sensation of different foods in my mouth, my stomach and textures. The smells and tastes were all too much for my brain to process at the speed required in school. Packed lunches were equally horrendous.

People always thought that I was lying to them. I remember one time at school I gathered my energy together to reply to a question about the colour of my parents' car. Ours was purple, but my teacher would not believe that it was possible to have a purple car. I froze and shut down at that moment. I wished that the ground would swallow me up because I knew that I was telling the truth, but I was being gaslighted again. I asked my mother when I got home what colour she would use to describe our car and she said purple. I asked her to speak to my teacher so that they understood I had not been lying. Unfortunately my mother did not understand why it was so important to me and dismissed my request, saying: "don't be silly".

It may be clearer to you now why I never felt safe growing up. I was unable to say what I was feeling or what I was experiencing, as I knew whatever I said would be dismissed as a lie or as me being silly. This "don't be silly" comment was far too often the response to any experience I shared.

I was essentially struggling to feel safe. Safe in school, safe at home, safe going out and safe playing with friends.

My coping strategy at school was to suppress everything that I hadn't understood so that when I got home, I would be like a big jack-in-a-box. I would explode and talk incessantly which led to my family telling me that I was "too much". It felt unsafe to express myself to them, so I stopped.

I learnt to hide in my room and create my own safe space. Reading became one of my chosen methods of shutting out the world in a way that allowed me to feel safe. I started to collect little things and keep them in special boxes. I can still, to this day, remember one thing that was in this special little box that would bring me such peace. I would never have used the word safe at that time, but it definitely soothed me and helped me to feel calmer.

A relative had given me a little perfume bag where you could keep a little perfume spritzer. I can visualise it and describe it as if it were here, in front of me right now. It was the most beautiful blue crushed velvet and the smell was soft and light. It had a little ribbon that was a deep red colour to tie it at the top. I loved it. I would put beads or a little doll in it.

At the time I didn't know or understand why this collection of special things was so important. I remember packing them if we went on holiday and checking time and time again to make sure they were there.

# WHAT I WISH I HAD HEARD

This was the one constant in my life, the one thing that was reliable because it was under my control at a time when nothing else was. I knew that no matter how I felt, my special things would be there.

I remember one particular outing with my parents where I took my precious rag doll and she got left behind. I felt huge amounts of grief and sadness that went on for days, weeks, months and even years. Of course the response from my parents was: "it's only a doll, get over yourself. It doesn't matter." But it did matter. It was so important to me that I felt, in some way, I had lost an arm. And as an adult I now understand that these constants were things that I built up to give me a safe place.

Over the years, I have discovered many tools and techniques that have helped me manage my neurodivergence. I have also met some amazing teachers who have shared their work with me, including Nanny Aut. She has developed a beautiful way of explaining the limbic system that I find really helpful. I wish this knowledge had existed when I was growing up. According to Nanny Aut, different parts of the brain do different jobs and here is an introduction to them:

Air Traffic Controller:

In charge of the central cortex. The Air Traffic Controller is responsible for logical decision-making, and deciding what is and isn't important for us to act upon.

When I was feeling stressed, distressed and anxious, I was responding to stimuli from a highly emotional place. This meant that I was incapable of anything requiring logic.

It is no surprise that my parents' logical responses were impossible for me to connect with; and why my emotional and sensory outbursts made no sense to them, for they were highly logical people. When triggered by my responses, they continued their logical response as perhaps they did not feel safe in a world governed by emotions. In some ways, we may mistake control for creating safe boundaries.

Panic Monkey:

One of the survival mechanisms in the limbic system. It's not in charge but can take over if there is a threat. The Panic Monkey keeps a lookout for all different types of danger. When it feels any signs of threat, it alerts the Air Traffic Controller.

I wonder if my Panic Monkey took over from my early years because I felt as if I was on high alert continually. Perceiving everything as a threat meant that I only felt that sense of safety when I was in an environment I could control, effectively only my bedroom.

Dino Brain:

In charge of the amygdala, the Dino Brain acts in defence to protect you in whatever way it feels is best. If Panic Monkey says there is a threat, then Dino Brain will act in any way it can to protect you, using any of these modes: ight, flight, flood, fawn, flop, or freeze.

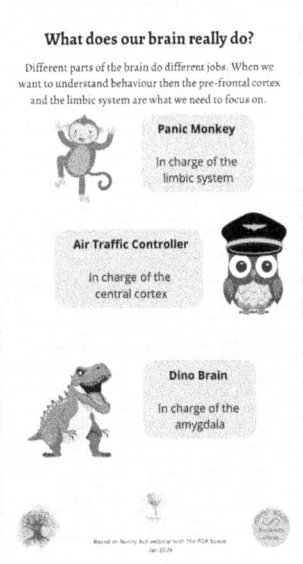

As I reflect upon my life experiences as a neurodivergent child, teen, and now an adult, I can see how I have used all of these modes at various times for different situations. I recognise how sensory overwhelm can still throw me into any one of these modes, despite the numerous strategies and techniques I use to reduce the impact of stressors in my life.

I have learned how to create safe space for myself and how to regulate my energy when I am able to anticipate a stressful event. I also know enough about my differences to plan and prepare well in advance, and to have strategies for overwhelm when it seems to jump out of nowhere.

I have learned so much more since realising that my own two boys are also neurodivergent in their own unique ways.

As a result, I set up The PDA Space to raise awareness and to make a positive difference for families across the globe. PDA is an abbreviation for Pathological Demand Avoidance or, as some prefer to call it, Pervasive Drive for Autonomy.

I am fortunate to be able to work and collaborate with many amazing parents, carers, and education and health professionals. This enables me to provide support to members of the community, so that they can gain access to the knowledge and information I never had, and make a positive difference for their own families and future generations.

This has been a very steep learning curve for me and my family. I am forever grateful to the friends and colleagues who have gently guided me to sources of support, provided advice and guidance themselves, and who continually hold space for me, as I do the same for the wider neurodivergent community.

I'd like to thank Karen Goodson for her support in being able to translate my jumbled voice notes into a readable chapter, and to acknowledge that even as an adult, I do still need support with communication in addition to other areas in my business.

# Life Lessons for Young Adults
# Clare Ford

*'The greatest glory in living lies not in never falling, but in rising every time we fall.'*
*- Nelson Mandela*

*Dedicated to my two gorgeous sons, Alex and Oskar, who have taught me so much. Thank you.*

Have you noticed, when we're on this journey called life, we often find ourselves racing, pushing or striving for more—sometimes because we genuinely want to, and other times because of deep-rooted fears and the insecurity that we don't want to be found out as a 'failure'.

In my decades of personal and spiritual growth and life experience, I've been through these scenarios multiple times, with a cycle that often repeated itself. So, if it's okay with you, I would like to highlight a few key pivotal moments of my life, hoping you might find strength from them and also learn how to break any negative cycles in your life, so that they aren't repeated decades later!

Let's start with my formative teenage years. When I was seventeen, I was bursting with ambition. I had my sights set on going to Oxford or Cambridge and I took on four A-levels and an additional AS level, together with the Oxbridge exam, stretching myself to the limit. Coming from a multilingual and multicultural family, I had chosen to learn multiple languages—the literature was an integral part of that, because I wanted to make my parents proud, to shine in the eyes of my teachers, and to prove to everyone—and most importantly, to myself—that I was doing everything I could to succeed. On top of that, I was working to earn money—Saturday jobs, holiday jobs and evening jobs. I did this to pay for driving lessons and buy myself a car, to go on holidays and experiences that would take me one step closer to the freedom I so desperately craved. I was also in a long-term relationship with a boyfriend whom my parents didn't approve of, adding extra stress and tension to the household and my life in general.

What started as ambition from being in a top grammar school soon spiralled into anxiety in sixth form college. I felt that if I dropped even a single commitment, I would be considered a failure. I had no adult mentors to advise me and the pressure became suffocating, leading to a myriad of mental health challenges including depression, paranoia, and an eating disorder. Like many teenagers, I sought refuge in the wrong places: alcohol, cigarettes and questionable friendships. I

# WHAT I WISH I HAD HEARD

was burning the candle at both ends going out, clubbing, under-age drinking—wearing all the hats: girlfriend, party-girl, high-achiever, financially independent, sporty, attractive, funny—and I was exhausted! Everything came to a head just before my A levels, when I fell seriously ill at college and had to miss some classes. I also had an operation on my ankle due to too much cycling (I was trying to save on bus fares) which meant that I attended my interview at Robinson College, Cambridge, on crutches. I failed my driving test twice, and therefore needed to pay for extra lessons and keep going until I passed. On top of all of that, my boyfriend and I were constantly arguing and it was getting harder and harder to see each other. He was Pakistani and there was a lot of pressure on him from his family to not see me for cultural reasons. You can probably guess the outcomes...

- I didn't pass my interview to get into Cambridge.

- I broke up with my boyfriend.

- I passed my driving test on the third go.

- I flunked my A levels, and had to defer a year for university.

Not exactly the 'go-getter', 'high achiever', amazing young person I had thought myself to be. And yet... there were important lessons which I needed to learn—life lessons, not academic ones, as a result of this striving, pushing and comparing. I began to understand that there is more than one route to success. The skills I learnt in my deferred year (where I retook some A levels and also did a bi-lingual secretarial course) actually earned me more money in the holidays, and I met some great people. I calmed down. I looked after myself better. I didn't have to prove myself to myself. I got into Reading University the following year, and actually going as a more mature student was a great help when it came to managing money, making new friendships and juggling the party/work/study/relationship plates.

Fast-forward to Clare at thirty-four—The Roller Coaster of Motherhood: I found myself as a proud mother of two wonderful boys... but old habits die hard. I was working part-time, tutoring, and managing household responsibilities. The joy of motherhood was sometimes overshadowed by the constant desire to meet everyone's expectations. I wanted to be the 'supermum' that everyone praised, the wife who had it all together with the perfect home, and the perfect daughter in the eyes of my parents. This insatiable quest for validation and high standards led me down the now familiar path of anxiety and depression.

Like many mums, I put a brave face on it—smoothing the cracks with foundation, getting up and out of the house, going on adventures with my babies and connecting with other new mums. But, as before, I was exhausted. Gruelling breast-feeding schedules, the worry of babyhood illnesses, working part-time and juggling childcare with very little adult support from my husband or family took their toll. But I still didn't ask for help. Not until I really needed to—when I was making mistakes like locking the car keys in the boot of the car or losing my house keys on a regular basis, putting us all at risk. This time, I turned to comfort eating and cigarettes to cope, and became addicted to coca cola! I also had horrible bouts of anxiety and panic attacks. So, what did this episode teach me?

- That self-care is paramount—I need to put myself first if I want to be able to look after others.

- That I should have asked for, demanded even, help and support earlier—other people aren't mind-readers.

- That no-one has any of this stuff figured out—and that's ok.
- That trying to be the best, to please others and to not put my needs first is my Achilles heel, and the recipe for disaster.

But, did I learn?

Clare at forty-two—Chasing Professional Dreams: By forty-two, I was deeply engrossed in my teaching career, but my ambition remained both a driving force and an Achilles heel. Balancing work, managing the home, tutoring, and raising my sons became a near-impossible juggling act. My headteacher's approval, feedback from students, and the weight of financial responsibilities made me push myself harder than ever. My husband was commuting to the city, which left me as the main carer for the boys, should there be any unforeseen hiccups at school. Again, I felt guilty asking friends for help—and had to pay extra for breakfast club and after-school club to stay open. Unfortunately, this incessant drive took its toll on my mental health and personal relationships, leading eventually (although perhaps unsurprisingly) to a breakdown in my marriage, a heart-wrenching divorce, and a suicide attempt.

So, what have these crises taught me?

Now, after many years working on myself, I have ditched the people-pleasing behaviour and am a happily reformed perfectionist, delighting in taking imperfect action for the joy of simply following my intuition and passions. But this does take courage and is not for the faint-hearted. It needs to be worked on—and, if you can work on yourself now, this may save you several decades of heartache.

It's interesting how life has a way of teaching us the same lessons repeatedly until we finally get it. My experiences, though painful, helped me understand a few core truths. I realised that my need for external validation was an endless cycle, and true validation can only come from within. Instead of constantly seeking others' approval, I learned to cheer for myself, listen to my intuition, and establish clear boundaries.

## 'The greatest glory in living lies not in never falling, but in rising every time we fall.' – Nelson Mandela.

I had to rise multiple times, learn, adapt, and change. I used some past-life hypnotherapy, tapping and timeline collapse to connect with my inner child at the age of nine, to see what she needed and to see if I could better understand the root cause of these patterns.

This is what came through for me:

Clare aged nine - The Silver Jubilee: I could hear Granny in the kitchen, preparing one of my favourite lunches—a juicy Fray Bentos pie with buttery Smash mashed potato and some green beans, topped off with beef gravy. I could see the tops of the trees swaying through the windows, high up on the eighth floor, and hear the soft rumbling of a plane, not far away, flying over London on the way to Heathrow. I used to like being at Granny's. She was kind and didn't shout or smack me, and took the time to play with me. We played all manner of card games, and simple games like dominoes and hide-and-seek; even if she was busy I used to enjoy colouring or reading. I was colouring in union jack flags for the Queen's special jubilee. I specifically remember one time, when I had gone into the kitchen to get a glass of milk, and accidentally dropped the glass milk bottle, spilling the pale white liquid all over the dark blue tiles. I looked at her, eyes wide with fear, expecting a torrent of shouting and a smack on the bottom with the back of a hairbrush for being such a naughty, stupid, clumsy girl. But instead, something amazing happened. My Granny just looked at me gently and said, "Don't worry. It's no use crying over spilt milk. Let's get this tidied up and get some more when we pop out to the swings later." I just nodded, mute, too choked with surprise to speak. Later on, after we had been to the swings and replaced the milk, we were playing Snakes and Ladders, and I asked Granny why she wasn't cross with me. She looked up in surprise."You're not naughty, Clareleo," she said. "You're kind and beautiful and funny and clever—and you're really good at learning and remembering things. It's okay not to know things and to make mistakes. You're only nine and you're still learning. There's no need to worry about the milk. It was just an accident—and everyone has accidents now and again."

I realise now, as an adult, that these are the words I still need to hear.

That these are the words my inner child still needs to hear. Because, so often, that critical inner voice (which sounds like my mother's) gets too loud... and so I withdraw inwards, becoming paralysed in my decision-making... fearful, stuck. And so, by meeting my inner-child, holding her close, telling her how much she is valued and loved, we rebalance, recalibrate and reconnect, in order to live again for another day and break free from the chains of the past.

<u>Key Takeaways for Young Adult Readers:</u>

*1) You are not alone.*

According to the American Psychological Association, almost 70% of teens feel significant pressure to excel in school, suggesting that many of you grapple with the same struggles I did.

*2) Never fear seeking help.*

People are there to support, understand, and guide you without judgement.

*3) You are always learning.*

Remember, life is a journey of loving, living, and continuous learning. It's perfectly okay not to have everything figured out. The universe has a funny way of reteaching lessons until we truly grasp them—I can certainly vouch for that! So, listen, adapt, and learn.

*4) Start now!*

Address and confront your inner critic and limiting beliefs. As you grow, this foundation will pave the way for a more fulfilling life. My journey, filled with peaks and valleys, has given me insights that I now cherish.

And while life is never without challenges, it's how we respond, learn, and evolve that truly defines us.

Sending you so much love x

# From Darkness to Light: Overcoming Childhood Emotional Neglect

## Kimberly Keane

*'Self trust is the first secret of success.'*
*- Ralph Waldo Emerson*

*To my supportive and loving husband, and my beautiful daughters, thank you for giving me the motivation and strength to keep going, and for always seeing the best in me.*

"**D**o you know you're being affected by childhood emotional neglect?"

"No," I replied. I was blindsided by yet another label as I sat across from my therapist. I was thinking—how did I go from a career-driven identity crisis, to even more negative concepts like codependency, anxiety, and now this?

As confused as I was, I was also relieved, because I was hoping that this discovery would be the final piece of the puzzle to getting rid of the dread, frustration, and desperation I had been experiencing since starting counseling.

As I sat there still reeling from the bombshell that was just dropped in my lap, my therapist asked me to close my eyes and focus on my breathing, because she had a meditation she wanted me to try. I felt nervous and unsure, since I was still somewhat new to the concept, and had a hard time stopping my relentless thoughts. I was willing to give it a try though and attempt to turn them off, since at this point, I had nothing to lose.

I put my feet flat on the floor and leaned my back against the maroon and plaid high back chair, feeling my heart thump in my chest while trying to breath as the meditation began.

Even though I felt shaken, I was excited and hopeful too, at the thought of getting to meet my inner child, Little Kim. I wanted to do right by her since so many others hadn't.

As the meditation progressed, I felt disappointed because all I could see was the color black—a vast darkness. Suddenly it changed, and there was a field of long, wavy, green grass and a beautiful blue sky with white fluffy clouds. There in the field was a little girl with long, blond hair sitting on a blanket. There she was! My inner child! My excitement quickly turned back to disappointment when I saw the little girl's face. It was my daughter, Lilly, when she was three years old.

When I shared this at the end of the meditation my therapist said the vision of my daughter probably came through because that was a child in my life that I could easily connect to, especially since she looked very similar to me when I was three years old. But I wondered if I'd ever connect with the Little Kim hidden somewhere deep inside of myself.

Despite not seeing Little Kim during the meditation, my therapist assured me that with some work she was sure I'd meet my inner child and be able to rekindle a relationship with her. She said my inability to connect with her during the meditation was because I had repressed my inner child so deeply, as a means of protecting myself and her, due to the trauma from my childhood.

I left that session knowing nothing about childhood emotional neglect, but was optimistic that in my upcoming sessions with my therapist she would share information to help me do the work to heal, while having grace and self-compassion. To my dismay, the guidance and support didn't come. As I had done previously with codependency and anxiety, I decided to learn everything I could. I was committed to doing whatever exercises and activities I could find as well as implementing any recommended strategies so that I could finally overcome all that I had endured, and move forward as quickly as possible.

I turned to Google and searched: 'childhood emotional neglect'. Among the millions of search results I found the work of John Bradshaw. He had so many resources on how to heal from childhood emotional neglect. The first one I turned to was 'Homecoming: Healing and Reclaiming Your Inner Child'. This was a book that opened my eyes to inner child work, which is a powerful tool for healing childhood emotional neglect.

As I cracked open the book, I didn't realize how deeply this work would affect me, and how tumultuous it would feel to do it. I thought it would be similar to how I was managing my healing journey so far. Yet as I dove in head first, it hit me so much harder than I imagined possible.

I was already exhausted from processing and trying to work through codependency and anxiety, along with my roles as a stay-at-home-mom and part-time adjunct college instructor. I was squeezing healing activities and exercises in between my younger daughter's naps, getting my older daughter to and from school, and her extracurricular activities. Adding inner child work to my already overflowing plate felt insurmountable. I knew I couldn't continue feeling like I'd reached the deepest depths of hell, because it wasn't allowing me to live the life I was craving. One that felt stable, calm, and joyful.

I also felt like I had been thrown to the wolves by my therapist because she was throwing labels at me left and right, without really giving me tangible methods for coping and managing them. She suggested I 'spray myself with invisible cooking spray to let the codependency slide off', and was also adamant that antidepressants were a good solution as they would give me the 'stairs to climb out of the metaphorical ditch', rather than trying to claw my way out each day. Unfortunately, I didn't have enough awareness to proactively 'spray myself' with invisible tools. Medication didn't feel like a good fit either because I knew the unhelpful beliefs that plagued me and the habits I was stuck in had to be unlearned. It was going to take time.

I didn't feel like I always had the support I needed from my husband. He was consumed with his demanding work schedule and trying to be present for our young daughters, since I was distracted by the emotional and mental overwhelm from working through the healing process of all the labels I now had to come to terms with. When he was home he didn't really know what to do to help me. Honestly, I didn't either and so it was hard to share with him what I needed.

After reading the first few chapters of 'Homecoming', a strong hatred towards my parents started festering. I also developed this same sentiment towards my grandparents, and all of the generations I'd never met, because this was a long history of dysfunction on both sides of my family. I learned that much of my experience with childhood emotional neglect, codependency, and anxiety stemmed from the generations of unhealed family trauma.

I couldn't stop asking myself, "Why would my parents bring me into this world?" Didn't they know they'd pass down their issues to me?

During all of this, I was also connecting with my spirituality. I wasn't raised to believe in a higher power, or to have faith that things would be fine when they felt rough. Instead, in my family, we put our heads down and barreled through until we were on the other side of whatever the obstacle was.

One of the concepts that came up while exploring spirituality was the idea that we all have souls—that our soul selected our physical, earthly being and incarnated into that life as part of its journey. I absolutely couldn't fathom why my soul would sign up for any of this.

None of it made any sense.

As this burning hatred seethed within me, I suppressed it. I didn't want to hurt or upset my parents or my family if they found out that I was feeling anything but love for them. I knew that childhood emotional neglect was not their intention and they were doing the best they could with what they had. Yet I couldn't understand how they didn't see it happening.

It's not surprising when I look back though, because my parents were in survival mode and managing life as it came for a large portion of their lives. Especially for my mom, since her childhood was wrought with heartache and hardships. They were most likely unaware their coping skills were deficient. They also hadn't sought the help of a mental health professional since this wasn't a normalized option for getting through painful, difficult experiences at the time.

What I didn't know at the time was that they couldn't see their own struggles and dysfunction. Often when we're in the thick of it, it's hard to see things for what they are. Had I known this way back when, I would have been able to understand things more clearly and better handle the ups and downs.

Not only was I hiding my feelings towards my parents and family, but I was experiencing immense shame and embarrassment. I didn't want anyone to know that I was doing inner child work or that I was in therapy. I was teetering on the brink, convinced that my life was never going to get better and this was as good as it was going to get.

As I did the exercises in Bradshaw's book, several pivotal memories resurfaced. One of the more severe times where I felt like I wasn't seen or heard was around my dad's upcoming marriage to my stepmom. I wasn't happy he was going to marry her. I begged him not to go through with it. I felt like she wasn't always very nice to me. Ultimately, I felt like I was being replaced and was no longer his main priority. He was steadfast in his decision and wouldn't change his mind. On top of it all, my dad shared my feelings with my stepmom.

I ended up in therapy. I remember very vividly sitting in the cold, wood paneled room, with the fluorescent lights buzzing and the therapist sitting across from me holding her notebook and pen in hand. I nervously played with my tissue, wiping away the tears as I shared what I was going through. I didn't get the reaction I was hoping for. I desperately wanted her to say that I was justified for what I was feeling. Instead, she told me that I didn't get a say in the situation because I was just a kid and it was an adult decision that eight year olds weren't part of. I had to accept that my dad was getting married and that this woman was going to become my stepmom.

Another memory that flooded back was from when I was around twelve years old. I wanted to take horseback riding lessons and attend a summer camp at a local horse farm with several of my best friends. This was not long after the actor who played Superman, Christopher Reeves, was traumatically injured in a horse-riding accident. My dad wouldn't allow me to take lessons because the serious injury of a 'legend' instantly meant it was a dangerous activity to participate in. Our compromise was that I could attend the camp and ride as long as the horse I was riding was being led with a lead line by an experienced instructor. I was not allowed to go any faster than a walk and certainly no jumping was allowed.

These memories reminded me that I often felt like I couldn't trust myself to know what I needed or what was right for me. It also reaffirmed why I spent most of my childhood trying to blend in like a chameleon, since I often felt like a burden for trying to communicate what I was thinking, feeling, and wanting. These behaviors and beliefs had carried into adulthood leaving me feeling much like I did throughout my childhood and into adolescence.

As I continued down the Google rabbit hole and worked through the activities in Bradshaw's book, the concept of reparenting kept appearing. It felt like a good fit and something that could be profound with helping me heal since it would allow my inner child and me to have new opportunities and experiences. It would also give me chances to express my thoughts, emotions, and desires in a way where I could practice with safe and supportive people in my life.

The emotional neglect most likely started around the time I was three years old, since this was when my parents' marriage was at its most volatile. Despite this, it felt more natural to start engaging with my inner preteen. This too was a turbulent period of my life filled with painful memories that were still so crystal clear. I could access and remember these memories more easily as an adult than the early memories of my toddler years.

Since horseback riding was something I wanted to do so badly and didn't have the chance to fully experience, I decided I was going to try it. Regardless of what anyone thought about how safe it was, how much it costs, or that I should be home on the weekends with my husband and daughters instead.

I went to the local saddlery store and purchased riding gear. I splurged and treated myself to a helmet and riding boots that I really liked rather than settling for the cheapest ones, despite not knowing how long I'd take lessons for or how often I'd go on trail rides.

I started with weekly lessons to get the basics down. I even tried trotting and thought it was invigorating! I couldn't get enough of being around the horses. There's just something about looking into a horse's eyes and seeing their essence looking back at you that had me hooked.

Since I realized I loved riding so much, and lessons just didn't feel like enough, I decided that I wanted to go on trail rides regularly as well.

I even took it one step further and made the decision that I wanted my young daughters to have this same experience. I signed the three of us up for a trail ride. I wasn't really sure what they would think of being on a horse. Not surprisingly, they also loved it. It was an incredible experience to be able to share my excitement with them and have them reciprocate it.

As I 're-parented' myself, I gave myself permission to experience simple things that weren't as significant as riding lessons, like the toothpaste I wanted to use, and the style of clothes I wanted to wear.

Picking clothes was always a struggle because I didn't have a lot of autonomy since my grandmother drilled her own fashion rules into my head. I didn't have a lot of freedom to express my own fashion sense under my stepmom and dad's supervision either. I was never able to independently decide what I liked.

The first clothing choice I made outside my comfort zone was buying a pair of ripped jeans. As a teen I wanted a pair desperately but was never allowed to own them. My parents and grandmother would remark that buying ripped clothes didn't look nice and were a waste of money.

I remember when I bought my first pair of ripped up boyfriend jeans how excited and terrified I was, all at the same time. I was excited because I validated my desire and was breaking free from the old programming. Despite being in my early thirties, I still worried what others would say and whether my family would object. I also thought I'd get weird looks or stares in public. To my surprise, no one gave me a second glance and there was no criticism from my family.

This gave me the courage to continue honoring and listening to my thoughts, emotions, and needs as I did more inner child work and 're-parented' myself.

My parents weren't always there for me in the ways I needed them, especially emotionally. This created unrelenting, deep feelings of not being enough, loneliness, and insecurity.

I couldn't count on them.

I knew that I couldn't get the validation I was so desperately seeking from them because that ship had sailed a long time ago. I was afraid that if I did try to turn back the hands of time to get what I lacked as a child, my parents still wouldn't be able to give it to me. I'd be back at square one. Maybe this is your worry too?

Relying on others will leave you in the same vulnerable place you were as a child. It's time to honor what your inner child didn't get but wanted so much.

You can do this by re-parenting yourself just as I did. You might be wondering how or where to start.

Begin by reflecting on your childhood. Were there hobbies or interests you wanted to pursue and weren't supported? Maybe it was a dance class, doing gymnastics, or taking art classes? Were there things you liked or wanted such as a pair of the trendiest sneakers or the latest haircut? It could even be a toy you wanted and you were told you couldn't have it. Was there a time where you needed a shoulder to cry on or a big hug because you were overcome with sadness? Create a list of everything that comes to mind.

After you've created your list, pick something from your list that feels like it would be easy to give to yourself. Select an item that isn't going to trigger any feelings of anxiety, fear, or overwhelm.

Also, allow yourself to feel all of your emotions as they come up. Don't stifle them. If you're feeling frustrated, notice what you're feeling in your body, what you're thinking, and how you're talking to yourself. Allow yourself to be fully immersed in the moment. The key is to acknowledge what comes up, feel what needs to be felt, but not stay stuck in it all. Having options to respond is helpful too such as journaling, taking deep breaths, or moving your body.

Once you allow yourself to experience what is on your list, you will develop more trust in yourself that you can meet your own needs in ways that feel right.

Re-parenting yourself and your inner child is not a sprint but a marathon. Patience, grace, and compassion will be important to practice to help keep any judgment, anger, or frustration you feel towards yourself at bay as you embark on this precious journey.

# The Day I Finally Chose To Evolve, Motivate, Inspire And Love You Emily

## Emily Nuttall

*'I now see how owning our story and loving ourselves through that process is the bravest thing that we will ever do.'*
*- Brené Brown*

*I dedicate this book to everyone who is on a brave journey of healing; of learning to understand and grow from their inner child, and finding themselves again through the pain and darkness. You are a warrior—be proud of who you are. You are loved, worthy and enough, and have something amazing and unique to offer this world. The light at the end of the tunnel is somewhere in sight. It will be a hard battle, but worth the fight.*

Ello teddy and bunny. Can you believe that I'm four years old now? What adventures we have been having lately, acting out lots of Disney fairytales together from the books Granny got me for my birthday. We get to have so much fun dressing up, drawing, being free, safe, and happy, not having to think about anything else that is happening.

If only our world together was the real world. That it would always be our 'happy ever after'.

At least when we're all together, you're not fighting with each other. There's no screaming or violence, physical hurt, emotional abuse or anger. I don't get shouted at or told that I am: useless, a mistake, unloved, a burden, a failure, stupid, ugly, fat, pathetic, or worthless. What do these words even mean? I try so hard to be a good little girl. I realise that I am a bit different to other children my age, but surely it still makes me worthy of love, safety and care, just like you give me all of the time?

I love it when you both hug me, protect me and make me feel how I should feel at this age: care-free, safe, imaginative, loved, wanted, and happy. If you could talk back to me, I'm sure we would have such special conversations together, full of joy and laughter. Oh, how I wish I could just wave my magic sparkly wand like the fairy-godmother in Cinderella

# WHAT I WISH I HAD HEARD

and make you come to life for real. Then you could then always hold my hands and help me run away back to Disneyland.

Sadly my envisaged image of my inner child in my own Disney World was no longer going to remain true. Only a few months earlier my dad walked out of the family home to live with his new partner. For months prior to this my mum and dad were shouting and violent towards each other. They were very unhappy when they were together, which I found very scary, confusing and lonely to process. But for me, Daddy was my father figure, my superhero, I was a 'daddy's girl' before he turned my world upside down. Still being so young and small, it just didn't make sense to me. I remember screaming at the top of my lungs: "did daddy not want me and Mum anymore?", "did he not love me anymore because I wasn't a 'normal child'?". Was it my fault that my happy family unit was being fully ripped apart?

I think when any child experiences the breakup of the family unit it can bring up many questions, thoughts, emotions, and behaviours. This is completely normal and expected. It's okay to have these feelings and emotions, and to need support, understanding and reassurance with this.

I know I had many challenges that my poor parents had to deal with from the very beginning of my life. I was a premature baby born eight weeks early, weighing a small 4lb 4oz. After a range of tests, scans and surgeon assessments I was diagnosed with cerebral palsy at one year old. This is a disability that affected my physical movement, development and some intellectual development. Later on in life, challenges happened as a result of injuries caused to my brain whilst my mother was pregnant. It involved a long journey of rehabilitation, physio, hospital stays, MDT meetings and many major surgeries to come.

Despite my feelings, I was too scared to show the fear, loneliness, confusion and sadness I was really feeling.

So many other difficult changes, adventures and opportunities then took place in my young life. Whilst some of these things were amazing, it was also terrifying to be growing up in a world full of so many unknowns ahead. With a mask of confidence I didn't show any fear, but when I was alone I remember the mask coming off, curling up into a little ball under the duvet, screaming: "this is all my fault. I hate everything about you Emily, including everything and everyone in my life". I would then go on to punch myself repeatedly in my stomach. I had turned into my own worst enemy.

With my mum adapting to being a single parent it brought about many new challenges for me. Mum had to suddenly take on everything alone in helping me to manage my disabilities, and the care I needed.

At night time I would hear her crying when she was alone. Four year old me just wanted to run to her, apologise, hold her and hug her; to somehow try and make all of this disappear like my fairy-godmother would in my imaginary Disney World. I remember screaming: "I'm sorry for everything mummy, for making all these horrible things happen, for being born as a horrible little girl".

With my mother now struggling to cope with looking after me, and having to go through divorce, other family members had to get involved. Then it was decided by the NSPCC that I should spend half of the week with my mother (this would have to involve extra family support), and half with my father and his new partner.

To help me on what I called 'Emily's enjoyable escapes', I would fill up my bright pink rucksack. Teddy and bunny would be put in the pockets on the side and in this bag would go my favourite colouring pens, paper, games and musical instruments, footballs, tennis balls, and my favourite sporting outfits.

With the amount I would try to cram in it was like I was moving house every week, but it was like a bag of magic coming to life in my 'whole new world'.

My gran was a very special role model in my life. She was a very petite little lady with grey curly hair, called Molly. She was an incredible, patient and caring primary school and music teacher. I trusted her with my struggles and challenges including what I would then go on to experience at my father's house.

The relationship with my own mother was broken. I was lost, angry, scared, and going off the rails, but Gran, with her calming nature and words was always close by like a guardian angel on my shoulder, hugging me. She would keep me safe making everything okay, and together with support services, she held everything together.

She took me into what I called her 'magical, musical, Molly moments', and it allowed me to always make such beautiful memories. We would put these memories in our 'Molly Memory Book' so that we could go back to these special reminders any time we wanted to.

My nan, Chris, was an energetic, smiling, fitness fanatic. She had very curly brown hair, and an infectious smile that would always make me feel better. She gave the best hugs in the world, allowing me to feel loved and comforted, just like I was being hugged by my brown fluffy teddy bear. Nan was patient and would listen openly, never letting me give up, no matter what the challenge may have been with my physical disability and mental health struggles. I always remember Nan wanting to give me new challenges to help me overcome adversity. Because of my cerebral palsy I still wasn't walking properly at this point. I remember I would always tell Nan: "Emily's embracing exercise through the bum shuffle show" and we would laugh our heads off together.

My aunt Meg was petite, but had a warming voice. She helped me to understand and make sense of the world. She encouraged and inspired my creative talents, helping me to develop into a confident, intellectual woman through writing, music, dance and art. Like my gran and nan she kept the family together, and me safe from harm, helping me achieve anything despite my challenges. Auntie Meg and I would love to go into our own 'magical, musical moments'. We would laugh together if the piano, guitar, or our singing sounded out of tune and I liked to put on shows for her. I called it making 'Meggie memories'.

Uncle Brian was another role model to me. He was my bright, bold, artistic uncle who created beauty through his artistic talents. He was known as 'Uncle B' and was the rock of the family. He loved everything to have colour and would help me bring my world to life through what I called 'Brian's brilliant books of drawings'. He would try to teach me to draw people but we would just end up laughing at my bizarre stick figures; but it was fun, it was bright, and it was beautiful in its own way (as he would always remind me).

Anytime I would visit those family members it was like being wrapped in a comforting safety blanket, full of love and joy. With no care in the world I felt like a proper little girl. These were the times I remember saying I am loved, I am safe.

After my father found a new partner, he decided to marry and she became my stepmother. From day one I wasn't accepted into her family. I wasn't really aware or understood what was happening, I just thought she was adapting to me coming into their lives, and maybe loving me in a different way.

As I grew up, I realised it was the start of emotional abuse. I always remember her dark black hair and scary eyes, and the look on her face. She would constantly scream at me every hour that I was there, telling me that I was worthless, ugly, fat, a failure, and a mistake, and that I had ruined her family. She would isolate me from my step siblings by keeping me in another room of the house. When I would visit, I would witness shouting, arguing and terrifying violence between her and my dad. It made my dad's house feel, at times, like a war zone.

My relationship with my mother had also finally started to break. We were always fighting, and I struggled to get on with her new boyfriend. I felt like a lost girl, trapped and at a crossroads, not knowing which way to turn. This made me more angry and broken.

I remember little me just pushing everyone away, screaming that everyone was horrible; saying that they just wanted to just destroy me even more. I remember screaming out: "I deserve to just be punished, I deserve to and want to die, that way this will all be made easier for myself and everyone".

How could a little girl who was so young even be considering this permanent way out of the pain? As part of having cerebral palsy, little me was always told that physical pain would be something that was constant due to the muscle spasms, pins and needles, and tightening muscles. I remember so many times when I would fall over on my wobbly feet and cut myself. I wouldn't cry or show emotions, I would just be numb and tell everyone I was fine. When I was unwell I wouldn't feel like eating which happened regularly with cerebral palsy and infections. I got used to feeling empty without food, and all the pain of what was going on around me would fade away, I would feel peaceful and safe, again telling everyone I was fine.

Now at twelve years old depression, anxiety, self-harm, suicidal thoughts and anorexia consumed my mind and body. My 'I'm fine' mask became my new best friend. I felt detachment and rejection, even with close loved ones I felt shame and fear. It was a violent war with myself of grief, despair, loneliness and loss, at this point.

At this stage no one knew I also had autism, and my 'overwhelm bucket' would fill up. I would be unable to express myself, experience meltdowns, and a downward spiral of detachment, numbness, anger, and fear. It was like a washing machine of emotions, and this led to more and more scary thoughts of self-harm. I attempted my first of fourteen unsuccessful suicide attempts at this age.

My role models were my go-to, just to run to them and to be held by them, but sadly they have all passed away now. All of their deaths destroyed my world. They were sudden, traumatic and unexpected. The grief is still so raw even to this day, that only now am I really starting to process, heal and feel it.

# WHAT I WISH I HAD HEARD

It was at the start of nine long inpatient admissions into mental health and eating disorder units that the voice in my head started screaming at me: "you don't need support and change, you just need punishment, pain and death". I was filled with loneliness and isolation, but somewhere out there I knew there just had to be some glimmer of hope.

I had to start to give my inner child and my current self lots of love and empathy by becoming my own compassionate best friend; helping others through my charity; volunteering, fundraising, speaking, training and coaching work that are facing similar struggles and experiences; by being brave enough to finally rebuild relationships.

I also deliver these in my training and lived experience roles to equip others with the skills and knowledge in these areas. I do this both for professionals and service users to have resilience in recovery, growing, and moving forwards so that they can be filled with hope.

As I now sit here on Tuesday 2nd January 2024, I reflect on my story and the journey of my inner child. I tried so hard to be brave and strong.

Becoming my very own best friend has been one of the most beautiful things in the world, and I have also made some of the most beautiful, empowering, and inspiring long-lasting friendships. I now have connections and opportunities that would not have otherwise happened if it hadn't been for my struggles and experiences. That is something I will be forever grateful for.

I have learnt that being honest and open was the bravest and most courageous thing to do for my inner child, and for myself now.

Talk to someone you trust, and don't blame yourself! Life experiences and recovery can be a roller coaster of a journey full of ups, downs, twists and turns, loop de loops, and backwards drops.

You can truly be proud of who you are, and know that you're not the bad things that happened to you. You can be anything you want to be. Just know that, no matter what, you are loved, worthy, enough, deserve to be alive, and have something truly beautiful and amazing to offer this world.

Please don't ever be ashamed of your inner child or of the painful struggles and experiences that have happened. They have made you the Emily that you are today. The bravest thing you ever did was continue to live when you wanted to die.

You haven't used self-harm now for over a year and have been eating disorder free for six months. After battling with these struggles for eighteen years, you have been suicide attempt free for the last year. That takes huge courage, bravery, and pain. Having to be vulnerable, ask for support, feel and heal isn't easy, but through all the treatment, therapy, and charity support you have empowered yourself in every possible way, and that is to be celebrated every single day.

> ***'I am brave, I am bruised, I am who I'm meant to be, this is me.'***
> ***- The Greatest Showman***

# Never Enough

# Kertrina Gearing

*'Life is not about waiting for the storm to pass.*
*It is learning how to dance in the rain.'*
*– Vivian Greene*

*Dedicated to my loving husband and four amazing children, who I adore. Thank you for always loving and supporting me through the good days and bad. To my family (especially my sister), my beautiful friends, to Ruth and all my fellow peer coaches, thank you for all your kindness, support, encouragement, and for seeing what I couldn't.*

Beep, beep, beep, the pips went signalling the change in lesson. Up she got and off she walked. This blonde haired, blue eyed, slightly overweight, incredibly shy and deeply caring fifteen year old girl walked, in her grey skirt and black blazer, through the outside walkway from one lesson to the next. The blazer was restrictive, the tights irritating but the most upsetting thing wasn't the clothing or the cold winter air, but the laughing voices behind her. The exaggerated mimicking of her walk, the tugging at her bag, the 'accidental' nudging and shoving as a group of teens walked behind her belittling every action and noise she made. The only relief, albeit it very temporary, was heading to another lesson, which only reduced the mocking slightly until the next lesson change over, or the looming lunch break.

Her only consolation was that it wasn't P.E., she would have loved to never have had to attend another P.E. lesson for as long as she lived. If being overweight doing P.E. wasn't bad enough, there was the stark reminder that no one wanted her. Consistently the last to be chosen, being the sideline reject that no-one wanted was humiliating. As she felt that crushing feeling of rejection and the familiar reminder that she wasn't good enough, she was sharply brought back to the current lesson in hand.

Well at least she had lunch time to look forward to... or did she?

As she walked around the perimeter of the school, through the entirety of lunch with her one and only friend, she tried her best to avoid them. Sometimes that worked, other times not. On more than one occasion she was ambushed by a mob of angry teens, screaming and yelling, threatening to 'beat her up'. What has she done? You might ask. Nothing, not a single thing—her mere existence was enough to upset some people and if that wasn't enough for them, any other lie they could think of would do.

She dreaded her only friend being off school. She was new and had left her old school behind. Alone, unliked and unwanted, she faced her new reality. Was today just a bad day for her? No, just a repeat of the days gone and many of the days to come.

That girl was me!

You see no-one actually hit me, nothing was physically broken, and I had no bruises to show. So, what did it matter? The constant digging away, the picking at who I was, at every level of my being, gave birth to a very mean inner voice. The 'you're not good enough' dialogue that came to plague my very existence. Not consciously at the forefront of everyday, but behind the scenes like a mean sidekick.

You see I managed to leave school having done well in my exams. I married a kind, loving man, who I adore and together we raise four amazing children. Like most people, we have had our challenges in life, but we got through them. I thought my school days were firmly behind me, that they had no part in my future, but without realising, I had taken them with me, wrapped up in the internal critic voice of 'I'm not enough, I'm not good enough'.

Yet despite how hard I tried, or how well people said I did, it still wasn't enough. A lifetime of blaming myself for everything that was wrong, for not accepting praise, for continually over committing, and chronically 'people pleasing'. Holding myself back for fear of rejection, purposefully playing small because I wasn't good enough. It even went as far as blaming myself for things like my autistic children struggling at school, and later blaming myself for my dad dying. He had terminal cancer throughout his body but if I was more, better or even remotely good enough, I would have been able to do something to save him. But I couldn't, I had let him down and he was dead because I wasn't enough. All these things served as reinforcement that that inner critic was right, that I was never and will never be enough, despite how hard I tried. Even through all this I still had no idea where this voice came from. I never once realised it was from my time at school.

One positive from having that inner critic, or so I thought, was it made me work hard. Striving to be better, to achieve more so that I could prove to that inner critic voice that maybe I was good enough. That if I tried harder, got better I could possibly one day be enough. I now know that was never going to be the case but back then it kept me trying. But the thing is when you have that inner critic voice, nothing you do, and no amount of striving or working hard, or going above and beyond will ever be enough. The only thing it achieved was leaving me exhausted and drowning in my ever growing, never ending to-do list, which I could never keep up with, only fuelling more reinforcement of my inadequacy.

As I mentioned before three of my four children are autistic, and as any SEN parent will tell you, fighting for support is exhausting and isolating. A constant battle and struggle! Long story short, I ended up creating a Facebook group to bring parents together, thinking it would grow to about fifty members at its peak. It grew and grew, and I realised I was far from the only parent struggling. I desperately wanted to help others, to do more, and I tried, but nothing felt right. I was blessed to meet an amazing lady online called Ruth Kudzi, who runs a company called Optimus Coach Academy. I wanted so badly to train as a coach, to officially have the skills to help families like mine to reduce some of their challenges.

At the time I thought that if I was a trained coach, I would somehow be enough to help others. But accessing training was never going to happen. As a low-income family, we didn't have the money for coaching, and I definitely did not have the money to train to be a coach. But Ruth saw something in me at that point, something I hadn't, and approached me to offer me an opportunity that would change my life forever. A gift I will be eternally grateful for—a professional level coaching diploma scholarship! I thought I was signing up for a skill I could use (which I got in abundance) but what I also got in the process was something so much more valuable: the opportunity to experience coaching in all its beauty.

Through my time training I received coaching, coaching that helped me gain clarity in many areas of my life, but I always felt as though something was holding me back. Something that meant that I couldn't fully be who I wanted to be, or achieve what I wanted to achieve. It always came down to a feeling of not being good enough.

One day I was asked a question that would take me straight back to that fifteen year old girl, to a place I thought I was free from, but that had secretly enchained me for years. "Kertrina, tell me what that's about?" Off I reeled my endless stories of self-created failure, the stories I had told myself to prove that inner critic right. Story after story until the real nugget landed, and out poured my school experience. As tears flowed, I realised that it was still very much a thing and that really surprised me. After spending some time reflecting, journalling, and processing, I began to realise the impact had been far greater than I ever realised.

The bullying may have given birth to that negative voice, but I had been the one who had continued to grow and feed it, for the decades that had followed. It had become ingrained in every part of me, a very real, imprisoning story that I had not only told myself, but had warped reality and redefined life experiences to reaffirm its truth.

*Could I have been wrong all along? What if I was enough? What if I had actually been enough all this time?*

Wow, what a strange concept at the time but one through coaching, journalling, and reflecting I have come to realise is true. Being bullied wasn't a reflection of me, hey I can barely even recall their names their significance in my life was that small. I genuinely have no grudge against them, in fact I wish them well. So why continue to hate on the victim? What sense does that make? I would never speak to anyone the way I internally spoke to myself, why on earth would I think it was ok to treat myself that way? If I had fed and grown that inner critic monster, it was down to me to shrink it back again. Now I won't lie, there are still days that the beast tries to rear its very ugly head and I am very much a work in progress. It may always be part of me and I accept it for what it is.

As I worked on shrinking that monster, I began to grow the belief that I could actually be enough to help others. My parent Facebook group evolved and continues to grow, and Autism & ADHD Parent Support UK CIC was born. That Facebook group became a community interest company, a not-for-profit organisation. The Facebook group itself forms part of our support services, which now currently supports over 18.3K people across the UK.

But something else happened too. I realised what a hugely powerful tool coaching is and how it makes a huge difference. What if I could take what Ruth had given me and help others achieve the same? I recently launched my second business, Kertrina Gearing Coaching, alongside my CIC. If it can make such a difference to my life imagine the ripple effect it can make by making coaching accessible to as many other people as possible.

Coaching isn't therapy, it doesn't focus on the past but can touch there, with the intention of helping you move positively forward. It's about trusting that you actually have the answers within, and helps you process your thoughts and dig away life's baggage to see more clearly. What's not to love about that, hey?

As I continue to grow my self-belief and work on keeping that inner critic under control, I have a message for my inner child.

If I could, I would wrap my weary, battle-scarred body, bruised, and battered from life's challenges, around that little girl and hold her tight. I would tell her that life is going to be one heck of a ride, the roller coaster to beat all roller coasters. There will be some truly amazing times and some incredibly dark ones too, happiness and uncertainty, but one thing you never need to question is that you are enough. You are more than enough my darling—and you always have been!

So, I ask you, what would you tell your inner child if they were in front of you right now? What do you need to say? What do they need to hear?

# I Wish I Had Known That I Was Not Alone

## Annie Hunt

*'Let the anger go, it's only hurting you & how you feel. Be at peace, send love, take action and you'll heal.'*
*- Annie Hunt*

*This is dedicated to my Mum, who has sadly passed away, you were my best friend, thank you for always being there to support me, I hope I do you proud Mumma.*
*Also, this is for any girl who feels like they are all alone.*

*If you feel different, if you dislike your body and feel like you're not enough, but want to be confident in this world—this is for you.*
*And this is for every girl who wants to have closure with their abuse, but doesn't know how.*

I was sexually abused at the age of 10, by a person I should've been able to trust. My life changed forever. The childhood trauma affected my confidence in so many ways, and as a result I always struggled with unhealthy relationships, body dysmorphia, lack of self-worth, negative thoughts, depression and anxiety.

Over the last 5 years, I have completely *transformed* my life in every area and want to help others to do the same. My vision is to instil confidence into young people that I never had; and my mission is to end mental health waiting lists with my *Phunny Book!*

LITTLE ANNIE

Hello, my name is Annie and I am ten years old. I love trolls, playing in my room with dolls and my post office, climbing trees and cycling all around the local roads on my bike with my best friend, and I absolutely love snuggling with my black cat, Felix!

So, the other day something happened to me that I am not really sure about. At the time I didn't like it, but I didn't know that it was wrong for it to happen. When I got home my mum told me that it was very wrong and we had to go to the doctors. They made me lie there with no clothes on, prodding me all over my body, really, really late at night. It was so cold in that room.

That day I had been with this old man who looked after me now and again. He smelt horrid. There was a really strong smell on his breath... I can only explain it as 'bleugh'.

I was swimming in his pool in the garden on a really nice sunny day. Then we came inside to his dark house and he sat me on the sofa and took off my towel. I wanted it back on because I was cold, but he wouldn't let me have it. Then he leaned over me and, eugh, he smelt so gross I could hardly breathe. His big body was towering over me like a big dark shadow...

When I got home I went up to my room. I didn't speak to my mum at all. She was asking me questions and I wouldn't answer her. I was just blank. Numb. I wanted to be alone so I went outside to the garage where I had my pogo ball (it looked like Saturn: a bouncy ball with a plastic platform to jump on). I just kept jumping and jumping and jumping and didn't stop. My mum somehow guessed there was something that had happened that day. She was just about to put me in the bath, but then realised that there may be something on me that we couldn't wash off yet. She called a number and that's when we had to go to the doctor.

I had to tell the police over and over what had happened that day. It was horrible having to go over it again and again. I know I got bits muddled up—in which order they happened, but I tried to remember it as best as I could. They needed this so that they could help to get him into prison so that he couldn't do it to any other child.

It was not nice. My life changed from that day. I was different. I had a story that I wasn't able to tell everyone. It was like it had to be a secret. I told my best friends. But really, they didn't understand what had happened. My teachers all knew… but then I left that school and started a new school, so no one knew again, and I FELT REALLY ALONE.

<u>YOU ARE NOT ALONE!</u>

Ever felt different? Ever felt like no one understands you?

Like you are different to everyone else around you?

Well, that was me. This was a 'secret' I could only talk about with my close friends. *But no one else, no one else.* I was embarrassed and ashamed to talk about it. But why?!

I didn't understand. It wasn't me who had done anything wrong!

No! *He* was the one who was wrong.

And now I have to live the whole of my life feeling completely different to everyone. The first time I was with a boy I really liked, I was trapped in this horrid nightmare and couldn't get out of it, having flashbacks. My mind was transported instantly back to that moment.

The abuser pleaded guilty. I was angry at the world for years to come.

I even wrote to the prime minister to ask why that man (my abuser) only got a year in prison for what he had done to me, but then got let out 6 months later! What on earth?! I got a letter in response from John Major to say the sentencing was going to be reviewed and that it would be longer in the future. And thankfully, true to his word, it has.

Ten years old, not even out of primary school. There was no sex education back in those days! I didn't even know what sex was! I didn't know what he was doing to me at the time.

I wish I had known what was safe, as opposed to what was inappropriate touching, when I was abused. Throughout my teens and twenties I wish I had known this too and set boundaries. Maybe this would not have happened to me, had that been the case.

It wasn't until I started writing this very chapter, that I realised why I feel so strongly about the importance of it at younger ages. Lots of people have strong opinions about kids learning about sex education too early. I totally understand why they are worried because initially, I thought the same thing, but then I realised that my child would be safer knowing what is right and what is wrong.

Please remember if someone, if *anyone* touches you, even if it's someone you trust *(or someone you love)* in a place on your body that you don't feel comfortable with, then that is NOT OK.

I wish I knew I was not alone. I wish I knew other girls my age who I could talk to, that had been through the same thing. Nowadays there are so many support groups. Have a look on Facebook for free online help and ask your local GP for face-to-face support.

I wish I had known there was lots of support out there for me too. To be able to just talk to someone: a therapist, a counsellor, a friend, a family member, it would have helped so much.

I wish I had been courageous enough to speak to someone at primary school, at senior school and university! I needed support, but I didn't know who I could speak to, or where I could go for help. I realise now that asking for support is a sign of courage, not weakness. It's the first step to healing. So, be brave and don't be afraid to ask for help!

I wish someone had noticed my screams for help. I was self-harming through secondary school. For some reason, I thought it would be a good idea to write on my arm with a compass. Bad idea. No-one told me this was self-destructive behaviour, so I carried on doing it. Unfortunately, it was, and is still quite common in teens.

I was obsessive before I got with a guy, and then possessive when I was with a guy. I had so many trust issues. Years later I found out that this is connected to my abuse—the feeling of being betrayed. How could I trust anyone I was with? I was so jealous all the time. It ruined every single relationship I was in. Don't make the same mistake as me.

I wish I knew I had body dysmorphia... and why. It's so sad to think that I thought I was so fat. I felt so fat because of my intolerances (I had no idea I had them, at the time), which caused me to have IBS (Irritable Bowel Syndrome).

I was not fat at all when I look back at my photos.

I wish I knew why I felt fat... Unbeknownst to me, the food that I was eating was making me feel fat and insecure. I now know that I have many food intolerances that made me bloated, which is why I felt FAT, insecure and uncomfortable all the time! I used to hold my stomach in, *all day,* because I thought everyone would notice my fat belly! I thought my bloating was normal. It took me until my late thirties to work this out and realise that I need to cut out or reduce certain foods. I wish I had researched it then, and found out about the FODMAP diet (a diet specifically aimed at helping with IBS.)

I really wish that I went to counselling and therapy...long before I was twenty-eight years old. I wish I had found someone I could talk to openly about it, but I was adamant I didn't need help. I would not listen to my mum saying that it might help me. I thought I knew best! I was stubborn, and was convinced that I had dealt with it. The truth is, maybe I wasn't ready to talk about it and I didn't want to go over it all over again. I guess I just carried on like it had never happened... but *it never went away.*

I wish I had known what a healthy relationship is. I had numerous unhealthy relationships because I believed that I had to give a man my body for them to love me. I did not care about me. I did not know how to love myself. In the words of RuPaul: 'how in the hell you gonna love someone else, if you can't love yourself?!' Never a truer word spoken! Believe that you are worth more and you will receive more.

I wish I knew when and how to ask for help. That's one of the hardest things I've found in my life, is to ASK FOR HELP. Or know *when* to ask for help. What I realise now is that you have to actually *acknowledge* that you need help. I did not know that I needed help. But I wish I had *asked.* I have had to learn how to accept help when it's offered to me. I find it really hard to do because I always want to be Miss Independent!

There are so many different ways to get help nowadays e.g. your local GP, online searches, global support groups (face-to-face and online), websites, specialists, coaches, counsellors, therapists, mental health centres, and practitioners.

I feel so old! We didn't have the internet in those days. I know! No internet! It's unfathomable now! The best website that helped me was MIND.

I wish I had known about self-help books. When I was at my lowest point in my twenties, I was literally bed-bound with depression and anxiety. I spent a week in bed. In this time, I read a load of self-help books that changed my life. There are SO many out there now that you just have to find ones that resonate with you. The one that I would highly recommend is, 'The Secret' by Rhonda Byrne. It has changed my life!

I wish I had known the signs of how my abuse showed up in my life in many different ways. It wasn't until I researched my mental health symptoms and had CBT (Cognitive Behavioural Therapy) many years later, that I realised the severity and impact it had on my *whole* life.

I was frequently ill. I was a binge drinker. I suffered with awful migraines and stomach pains. I had mystery illnesses that would leave me bed-bound for days. I was diagnosed with severe depression on a few occasions. And I had debilitating anxiety. I literally couldn't get out of bed or off the sofa, which now I know, was actually due to the negative thoughts going round in my head. Like I was worthless, useless, not where I should have been in my life. The feelings of guilt poured out of me.

This was my lowest point. And I couldn't go on like this any longer. *This* is when my life started to change... because I WANTED TO CHANGE! *And my life started transforming!*

Mindset Exercises

These are for you to try if you are suffering with, or have experienced abuse.

I wish I had known the power of writing a letter! I didn't realise that this simple exercise could lift the weight off my shoulders.

1. I wrote a letter to my abuser BUT I did not send it. I wrote *exactly* how I felt. I got all of my anger out and every single emotion that I had towards him, that had been pent up for twenty years! All the swear words came out in that letter!

2. And then, I wrote one back from him how I wished *(not how I thought)* he would respond to my letter. I'll repeat that—*NOT* how I think he would have responded but what I wished he had said to me. This got so much out of my system.

And coincidentally, just a few months after this, my abuser was taken into rehabilitation and I was asked to go and see him to help his recovery and ultimately my closure. I got the acknowledgement and apology that I'd asked for in the letter I wrote! I couldn't believe it!

*This was a pivotal turning point of my life.*

So if you have experienced abuse, or have any type of conflict going on in your life, try this exercise. Make sure you're in a safe space and feel ready to do so, and see what happens for you! It's magical!

I wish I'd written more about what had happened to me. I did write some poems and songs when I was in my twenties, but I wish I had carried on writing about how I felt more. Because I knew that a part of little Annie's life was no longer there, my innocence was taken. I wish I'd known how powerful journaling is. Just writing things down and getting them out of my system has been so therapeutic.

*If there is one thing that you get out of this chapter, I hope that you write down how you feel.* Try it now! Just write down what you're thinking or feeling.

I forgive him, but I will never forget

I wish I had known how my negative thoughts affected me. After all of these exercises, therapy and counselling, I was finally able to let go of any negative feelings towards him that I had. All they were doing was hurting me, staying stagnant in my body and making me poorly, stopping me living my life.

*My REVELATION:* I was struggling mentally and physically because of *my own* thoughts.

*I hope that you can forgive someone for something that they did to you... for your own peace and good health.*

Thank you for reading this. Writing this chapter has been very cathartic and healing for me as I've written about my abuse in detail (not all of which I have included here). Going back over it is the hardest bit, but also the most helpful in the healing process. The counselling sessions connected to this book have been extremely helpful too, with many revelations about my childhood.

I hope that you have gained something from reading this. I hope it's helped you in some way to move forward with your life, positively! I hope that something I said clicked with you, and that you're able to ask for help, find support or cope with something you didn't before you read this. You can easily transform your life for the better with your thoughts! If I can help one person to do that, then writing this has been so worth it.

Annie's Mindset Hacks for you!

*I wish I had known all of the MINDSET tools* that I use today (which you can find via the link in my bio).

This is my unique method - My 5 "A"s are these:

- The best way to heal, or improve your mindset is firstly to *Acknowledge* that you need help.

- Then, you will start to become clearer and more *Aware* of what you need help with.

- The next step is to take *Action* to help yourself.

- Then you have to find a way to become *Accountable* to take that action!

- And when you *Accumulate* all the resources and skills you need to help you...

You will see a transformation in yourself, your mindset and your life!

# Author Bios: Cassie Swift

Find out more about the authors and how to connect with them here:

Cassie has been described by her children as 'awesome, kind, incredible, caring, beautiful, and 'AMAZEBALLS'. Her friends describe her as a kind-hearted, loving, and courageous woman and single mother of three. She stands up for her beliefs and the rights of others.

Cassie works as a family empowerment guide, specifically for teens, to enable them to feel empowered about life. She helps them to manage big emotions in a positive way, accepting the true version of themselves. As a result she brings calm and happiness not only to those she works with, but to the whole family. She is trained in several holistic approaches, including NLP, EFT (including teen specific EFT), and hypnotherapy as well as a lot of life experience, which helps her to put her unique spin on things.

Cassie is also a #1 best selling author of seven books, two which she co-created, as well as the founder and organiser of the Children's Mental Health Matters Summit. She has appeared both on the radio and in six regional newspapers speaking about issues surrounding children's mental health.

"Helping others, especially children, is my passion. I want to empower as many children as I possibly can!"

https://linktr.ee/CassieS

# Jill Nicholson

Jill Nicholson is a BACP accredited counsellor, clinical supervisor, trainer, and co-founder of Rapid Imprint Resolution Therapy which combines Transactional Analysis and EFT. She has a Bachelor of Education, an advanced diploma in Counselling and Psychotherapy, and is an accredited coach.

She started training as a counsellor in 1998 and spent the next eighteen years in the charitable sector, initially working with mums affected by postnatal depression, and latterly, running services in Edinburgh for recovering substance users and their children.

During her training Jill experienced counselling herself which was the first time she connected with her inner child and past trauma. Then her own healing journey truly began. That life changing and heart soothing experience created the foundations of how she works with clients today. Helping the adult by healing the inner child has become Jill's life purpose.

She currently resides near Edinburgh with her husband Paul and works with clients and students via zoom.

https://linktr.ee/jillnicholsoncoaching

# Kari Roberts

Kari Roberts is a Professional Accredited Parent Coach.

A seasoned parenting expert dedicated to empowering parents and fostering confidence in their unique parenting styles. With over fifteen years of professional experience coupled with the invaluable wisdom gained from being a mother of three and grandmother of ten, she understands the intricacies of family dynamics and the vital role parents play in shaping the emotional well-being of their children. Firmly believing in empowering parents to find their own rhythm in parenting without compromising the spirit of any family member. Her mantra is simple: "Start with you and watch things fall into place!"

Encouraging parents to prioritise self-care, emotional well-being, and self-discovery, recognising that a confident and emotionally secure parent forms the cornerstone of a thriving family, providing a solid foundation for the development of mentally healthy minds.

https://linktr.ee/kariann2309

# Emma Starling

Emma Starling is a Subconscious Transformation Expert, business mentor, author, trainer in Emotional Freedom Technique, and founder of Evolved Energetics™. She is also the founder of the Evolved Energetics Academy™: a world-class energy work, training and certification provider, that empowers healers, coaches and wellness professionals to spread their own healing ripple, by focusing on education, embodiment and evolution.

She lives in North Lincolnshire where she can be found roaming amongst the many woodlands, petting any dogs that will let her, and spending time with family. **Emma is passionate about** spreading the healing ripple and goes live every weekday to teach people how to do basic EFT for free.

https://campsite.bio/emma_starling

# Nicola Reekie

Nicola Reekie is a parent of a child with PDA (Pathological Demand Avoidance or 'Pervasive Drive for Autonomy'). Her mission is to raise awareness of PDA and make a positive difference for families across the globe. She's a solution-focused therapist supporting parents and professionals with their emotional well-being, and helping to create calm in often challenging situations.

Nicola is the founder of The PDA Space— a community for parents, carers, and professionals to share their experiences, strategies, and information about PDA. This includes supporting families, and those working with children and young people who are neurodivergent, and have an autistic/PDA profile. She works and collaborates with many amazing parents/carers, education and health professionals to provide people with more support.

https://linktr.ee/nicolareekie

# Clare Ford

Clare is an award winning international author, speaker, coach, healer, educator and parent. She is passionate about ensuring that children and teens are 'switched on' learners, accessing their natural gifts, abilities and talents to discover their true potential and live purposefully. Founder of Switched ON! the global online academy, and an academic coach with over twenty years' experience, Clare combines her unique skill set using her SWITCHED ON! Learning Method to unlock the brilliance in your child, tween or teen.

https://linktr.ee/switchedonacademy1

# Kimberly Keane

Kim Keane is a certified life coach, EFT practitioner, Reiki master, and sound healer. She is also the host of the One of a Kind You Podcast. She has addressed community organizations, women's groups, schools, and colleges, such as: Boys' and Girls' Club, Purdue University, Polka Dot Powerhouse, and Moms Who Dare. She strives to empower women to embrace who they are so that they can step into their light, and break free from the chains of their past.

https://linktr.ee/kvkeane

# Emily Nuttall

Emily Nuttall is a lived experience worker, coach, speaker, campaigner and trainer in autism, mental health, disability education, social care, suicide, self harm, and eating disorder services. She is also a co-author of seven books and an active volunteer speaker and fundraiser for many charities.

Emily is a trained adult and youth mental health first aider, and has completed domestic violence awareness training. She is all about empowering people and inspiring long lasting change. Her motto is: we are all brave, all bruised, and all who we're meant to be. By being different we succeed together.

https://linktr.ee/emilyn93

# Kertrina Gearing

Kertrina is a wife and mum to four amazing neurodivergent children, an assistant brownie leader and an avid allotment lover. She is most happy when covered in soil after a day at the allotment, when her fibromyalgia allows. She also runs her own not for profit organisation—Autism & ADHD Parent Support UK CIC, supporting parents of autistic/ADHD children from all around the UK.

In 2022 she began training as a life coach, and in early 2023 she completed her professional coaching Diploma. After training initially to support the parents she works with, she found it led her on the self-discovery journey of a lifetime, and thus her second business, Kertrina Gearing Coaching, was born.

Alongside the CIC work she also now helps women discover themselves, helping them to create their own version of authentic success in their life or business. She specialises in supporting other heart led, female entrepreneurs/business owners, to gain clarity, direction and purpose and turn their passion into success.

https://linktr.ee/Kertrinagearing

# Annie Hunt

Copyright: Legends Photography

Annie Hunt is an artist and a Transformational Mindset Coach specialising in Therapeutic Art and Cognitive Behavioural Techniques (CBT). She's forty-two years old with three kids: Reuben (nine), Beatrice (seven), and Beau (two) and is married to the man of her dreams, Matt. She's a full time mumma to her toddler with her own coaching business, Mindset Hacks, that she's been running from her home since 2020. And she also works at her local youth centre, because building confidence in teens is so important to her.

Annie wants to share with you the most powerful exercises that have helped her to forgive and let go.

https://linktr.ee/themindsethacker

www.ingramcontent.com/pod-product-compliance
Lightning Source LLC
Chambersburg PA
CBHW061749070526
44585CB00025B/2845